Praise for *Free Time!*

In this new book, Vajragupta takes us on a tour of time in the light of Buddhist wisdom. He starts by pointing out the ways in which our subjective experience of time relates to our states of mind. Grasping and aversion change the pace of experience and the generosity with which we engage the world. He explores clock time and the changes in the cultures, technologies and economies of time over the last centuries. Reflecting on the three lakshanas, or marks of being, in Buddhist thought, he asks the fundamental question of how we can develop a healthy relationship to change. What sense of self do we invest in? What are our stories and the attachments they engender? Are they true? Are they liberating? The book is easy to read, dealing with tricky philosophical issues in an accessible and enjoyable way and packed with everyday wisdom. You'll find moving examples, fragments of dream and metaphor, anecdotes from Buddhist practice, and resources for reflection on your own times and mind. It's a delightful and insightful read. – **Dhammamegha**, Buddhist practitioner and author of *The State of Secularism*

Today we're all familiar with time-stress – how can Buddhist practices help us cope with it? What does Buddhism have to teach us about our experience and understanding of time? Vajragupta's new book offers fresh perspectives on a problem that continues to worsen, and original ways to address it. – **David Loy**, Buddhist teacher and author

D1508185

According to Socrates, philosophy begins with a sense of wonder. The starting point of Buddhism, by contrast, is the experience of suffering, and the Buddha's overarching concern was its alleviation. In this fascinating book, Vajragupta combines the two: his discussions of time evoke a sense of wonder, but he also shows how our relationship with time can either entrap us in suffering, or release us into 'an expansive freedom'.

Vajragupta's discussions of time are very stimulating. Just what *is* time? We *think* we know of course, we take it for granted, but he points out that we don't *really* know. It's a deeply mysterious phenomenon, but that only becomes clear as we look into our experience more closely.

But this is also a practical book, pertinent to the Buddhist project of alleviating suffering, and the connection is the mind. Mind and time are not two separate or separable phenomena. Our states of mind determine how we experience time, and, conversely, the way we experience time conditions our states of mind.

Vajragupta's new work is refreshingly original, beautifully written, and crystal clear. Although the book isn't long, it took me some time to read because on almost every page there is something to reflect on. In fact, I can't remember the last time I read a book that yielded so many insights. Go and get yourself a copy as soon as you have some time. – **Ratnaguna**, author of *The Art of Reflection* and *Great Faith, Great Wisdom*, and co-founder and director of Breathworks

Vajragupta's book offers deep insight into untangling the frenzy of time. We're all caught in the accelerating currents of time, surrounded by labour-saving devices that paradoxically rob us of the free time we desire. His suggestions can provide a positive life change with less time stress. Clearly a book worth reading. – **Stephan Rechtschaffen**, MD, author of *Time Shifting*, a founder of Omega Institute and Blue Spirit Costa Rica

As someone who suffers from chronic, clock-watching, inbox-obsessing busyness, I found this a challenging, but ultimately inspiring, book. Vajragupta starts with the idea that we create our own experience of time, through either craving our current experience (which speeds it up) or aversion to it (which slows it down), meaning our relationship with time intimately reflects the quality of our lives. Critiquing the popular idea of 'living in the moment', he emphasizes that we need dreams and aspirations for possible futures, provided we do not become fixated on their eventual achievement. I revelled in how he dealt with the apparent paradox of (a) seeking a feeling of unbounded time, while (b) simultaneously acknowledging the need for prioritisation. Hints for experiencing timelessness, and stories of both contemporary acquaintances and the life of the Buddha, make it all very human and accessible, firmly rooted in experience. This is an excellent book, and I just hope it will improve my own relationship with passing time. – **Sir David Spiegelhalter**, Centre for Mathematical Sciences, University of Cambridge, UK.

Free Time!

from clock-watching to free-flowing, a Buddhist guide

Vajragupta Staunton

indhorse Publications

Windhorse Publications
17e Sturton Street
Cambridge
CB1 2SN
United Kingdom
info@windhorsepublications.com
windhorsepublications.com

Typeset by Ruth Rudd
Cover design by Katarzyna Manecka
Printed by Bell & Bain Ltd, Glasgow

British Library Cataloguing in Publication Data:
A catalogue record for this book is available
from the British Library

ISBN: 978-1-911407-23-2

Space and time are part of my mind. My mind contains space and time... The ten thousand things are condensed into the space, as it were, of a cubic centimetre, filling the mind. Flowing out of it, they fill the whole of time and space.

Lu Zhiu-Yuan (1138–91)[1]

Contents

Contents

About the author

Vajragupta Staunton was ordained into the Triratna Buddhist Order in 1994. Since that time he has been director of the Birmingham Buddhist Centre from 1997 to 2005, and director of the Triratna Development Team (helping to support a network of about fifty Buddhist centres across Europe) from 2006 to 2014. These days he lives as a 'wandering Dharma farer', spending periods of time teaching and helping out at different Buddhist communities around the world, and also making time for writing. *Free Time!* is Vajragupta's fifth book; it follows on from *Wild Awake*, a book about the practice of solitude in wild and beautiful places.

Acknowledgements

I would like to thank Pippa and Sam Armstrong, Aryatara community, Richard Dell, Andy and Catherine Gorno, Manjupriya, Phil Marston, Nibbhaya, Sagaradana, Tejapushpa and Tom Lostday, and Vaddhaka for accommodating me during different phases of the writing of this book. Thank you Dhivan for some comments on an early draft of chapter 1, which pointed me in the right direction. Thank you to Richard Dell, Dhammamegha, Matthew Hibbert, Indradhanu, Kalyacitta, Nibbhaya, Prajnabandhu, and Krista Tomson for your valuable feedback on the first draft. Thank you also to Akasajoti, Amaladipa, Samanartha, and Bridge Williams for so generously sharing your stories. Thank you Ratnaguna for the opening quote and for sourcing one of the Pali-canon stories from the Buddha.

I want to acknowledge the influence of Rob Burbea's *Seeing That Frees* on my approach in chapter 8, and also part of chapter 10. I could not have written the book at all, were it not for my teacher Sangharakshita, from whom I learnt the Dharma. Sometimes I have had the experience of writing a paragraph and feeling rather pleased with what I had come up with, only to realize that I had quoted (subconsciously, and sometimes almost verbatim) from his writing and teaching. Any mistakes in what follows are my own responsibility, however.

Acknowledgements

Thank you to all the team at Windhorse Publications for the good work you do. I am also very grateful for the editorial input of Cynthia Troup. Her suggestions have significantly improved the clarity and flow of the book, and I have learnt a lot from her. Thank you also to Dhatvisvari for her highly skilled copy-editing.

Publisher's acknowledgements

Windhorse Publications wishes to gratefully acknowledge a grant from the Triratna European Chairs' Assembly Fund and the Future Dharma Fund towards the production of this book.

Windhorse Publications also wishes to gratefully acknowledge and thank the individual donors who gave to the book's production via our 'Sponsor-a-book' campaign.

Introduction

I have always had a restless, anxious side, an obsession with the future. A couple of years ago I dreamt about being in some kind of borderland, a port or harbour. A long queue of articulated lorries waited, perhaps to drive on board a ship. There were crowds of people, some in groups milling about chatting, some also queueing by the lorries, and groups of children playing. The scene was busy, somewhat chaotic, but mainly good-natured and peaceful.

Suddenly a character emerged from the background, riding on a quad bike that towed a trailer piled high with junk. He pushed through the crowds in a mad hurry. He was wearing black biker leathers and had long curly hair. His staring eyes were large, bulging, and startlingly intense. He was determined to reach the front of the queue. He seemed oblivious to everyone else, and to how dangerously his bike was weaving in and out of the groups of adults and children.

He then parked his bike at the front of the queue and proceeded to try selling the odd assortment of items on the back of his trailer. It really was junk; trying to sell that stuff seemed rather desperate and crazy. People were also now complaining angrily to each other about how reckless he had been. But he seemed unaware, separate from everyone else.

In the dream I was one of the people in the crowd and, whilst the turmoil had been unfolding, I had realized that I recognized the crazy biker. I knew who he was. And so I offered to go and have words with him. When I tried to speak with him, however, he deliberately turned his face in the opposite direction. 'Please talk to me', I said, 'Don't you remember me?' Only then did he turn and look at me. And at that moment I woke up.

Who was he? He was, of course, me. As well as being an observer in the crowd, I was also the crazy biker man. Those two characters were representing different aspects of my psyche, the one trying to talk to the other and come into a better relationship with him.

That crazy biker man was always in a hurry, constantly trying to get ahead, pushing and rushing to the front of the queue. Head down, gritting his teeth, staring ahead whilst hardly seeing what was immediately around him, he became cut off from other people. When reflecting on the dream back then, I realized that I could be like the biker man. I saw how my restless striving was partly about proving myself, justifying myself by being seen to be making things happen. What I was engaged in at any given time was just a means to some future state. I thought that the quicker I could complete it, the sooner I would arrive at that bright future. Therefore I pushed at the hours, days, and weeks, and that pushing had gradually become an entrenched habit.

I am exaggerating to make a point. There were also positive motives behind that proactive and ambitious side of my character. Nevertheless, inwardly, there was a near-constant tension, as though inside me was an athlete on the starting blocks, bent forwards, muscles straining, pumped with adrenaline, waiting for the starting pistol to fire. My mind was nearly always leaning forwards into the future, planning the next thing and then the next thing, calculating how I could fit the maximum useful activity into the space of the day. Repeated over years, that leaning forwards had become part of my inner 'posture', a strong tendency or inclination, a weight always heavy on my shoulders. I felt what the *Sūtra of Golden Light* refers to as 'the oppression of the fleeting mind [...] the oppression of time'.[2]

On other occasions, however, my experience was completely different. Particularly when immersed in more wild and beautiful landscapes, I found I could stop, rest, and experience a deep ease and contentment. One of the characteristics of this experience was that I forgot about time. No longer was I constantly ratcheting up the future. This meant the present loosened too, opened out, and deepened into a rich, brimming fullness.

Noticing these stark contrasts, I became increasingly interested in my relationship with time. I saw that I viewed time as an external container, into which I tried to stuff as many activities as possible. The result was that my time had no flexibility, and I had no room for manoeuvre. I felt that I never had enough time. This also meant not having enough time for other people, for closeness and connection, for seeing what other people really needed.

I began to understand how time isn't something separate from us; the state of mind we live in also creates our experience of the time that we live in. Depending on my mental and emotional state, time would tighten or loosen, race or crawl; it became more hard and solid, or more fluid and flowing. And the more I looked, the more I saw just how deeply and fundamentally mind and time are interconnected, mutually dependent. How I lived created the time I lived in: time in an urgent arrhythmia, or time whose pulse was more easy and natural.

In our fast-moving world, many people can feel their time is wound tight, their lives constantly hassled and hectic. Fast-forward seems to be the collective default setting. So often we can be overbusy and overstimulated, and this can send stress levels higher and higher.

I have come to believe that investigating our experience of time, and considering our relationship with it, can be deeply and powerfully transformative. Noticing the feel and texture of our time can help us see more clearly, and understand more profoundly, the anxiety and restlessness that so often dominate our minds.

This book explores time from a number of different angles, in order to see how we can have a more healthy and human relationship with it. The first three chapters look at our actual day-to-day experience of time. The middle section of the book uses a variety of Buddhist ideas and practical teachings in order to explore what time really is, helping us to 'do time' in a way that is not oppressive and restrictive, but more free and flowing. The final chapters draw all the themes of the book together and consider what a fully transformed relationship with time might look like.

There are also extensive endnotes. Sometimes these point you to a text or other source I have drawn on, sometimes they define words or terms I have used, and occasionally they add a bit more information, or extend what is being said in the chapter concerned. At other times (particularly with chapter 9), I have used the endnotes to explore potential objections to my argument, and to answer those objections without making the main text too cumbersome and convoluted.

Part I

What's our experience of time?

The waiting room

'If you take a seat through there, the first chapter will be ready for you shortly.'

In the room are chairs upholstered in a rather lurid orange and brown tartan pattern. I sit down and wait. I note that there are six other people already in the room. A twinge of dismay sinks through my body; I am obviously not the first in the queue.

Two of the people have their heads bowed over their smartphones. Another is reading a copy of *National Geographic*. The room has beige carpet tiles and there is a wooden coffee table in the middle, almost hidden under a pile of dog-eared magazines: *Good Housekeeping, Country Life, Woman's Own.*

A woman mutters to her husband that they will have chicken casserole tonight. The husband is looking down at the floor, lining up the sole of his boot against the edge of the floor tiles.

Suddenly the door opens and everyone looks up hopefully. There is a palpable lift in the atmosphere. Then a voice calls: 'Janice Blackwood'. Janice is a woman in a pale blue jumper who springs nimbly to her feet. Looking pleased with herself, she scuttles out of the door.

Amongst those of us left in the room the atmosphere deflates again. Nobody speaks. I hate waiting. The husband of the chicken-casserole woman is now measuring the width of a floor tile against the sole of his other shoe.

On the wall there is a print of a watercolour painting by a local artist. There is a board covered with posters and notices pinned up untidily. I have read every notice at least three times. I can hear the phone ringing in the office and voices from down the corridor. The voices sound casual and chatty, which, for some reason, is slightly irritating. I look at my watch. Why is it taking so long? I hate waiting.

The door opens again. The receptionist leans into the room and looks straight at me: 'If you would like to come this way please. The first chapter is ready for you now.'

1 o'clock

Flexi time

We tend to think of time as uniform and linear, but, if we look at our actual, inner experience of time, we see that it stretches and contracts. Time goes at a quick march or else at a snail's pace. It shifts gear; it accelerates and decelerates. Time has texture; it can feel gushing fast or dripping slow, smooth flowing or stop-start staccato, tight and constricted or relaxed and open, satisfyingly deep or frustratingly shallow. Our *idea* of time is of something regular and even, external and objective. But our *experience* of time is variable and uneven, inwardly felt and subjective. Time concertinas. Time is elastic.

In some situations time seems to pass more quickly; it flies by too fast, and it seems like time itself has contracted and tensed up. Feeling we don't have enough of it, we end up racing time, up against time, in a fight with it. We may struggle to keep our heads above the water, desperately trying not to be swept away by the rushing tide of time. In this speedy mode of functioning, it is harder to have time for other people; we can become less patient, less connected to others. Perhaps this experience of time is increasingly common in our consumerist, technological, and highly sophisticated society. Many people's work lives seem busier, faster, more driven and stressful. If every hour of every day in our diary is chock-a-block with meetings, appointments, activities, social engagements – even good and worthy ones – the result is a constant rush. If we fill to bursting all our time, we end up feeling we have no time. Consequently, our lives may feel tight and constricted, bitty and superficial, as though we are slipping over the surface of our days, trying desperately to stay upright.

At other times, however, time can drag dully by. There is too much time, and we wish it would pass more quickly. Perhaps, for some people, their work is undemanding and repetitive; perhaps there isn't enough in their lives that seems meaningful and creative. Or perhaps we're on the rebound from overbusy time, tired and exhausted and unable to concentrate or engage with anything more deeply satisfying. Maybe we find ourselves confronted with work and tasks that we resist and would rather avoid. We're bored and we wish the time would pass. Time seems slow, sluggish, and stagnant. It feels empty and hollow, and we feel inert and lifeless. We wish we could kill time, and so it becomes dead time: time that we want to bypass, to get out of the way. And then, to kill time, do we sometimes waste time? Can we distract ourselves with trivia, or lose ourselves in mindless fantasy, or keep ourselves busy and occupied just in order to escape time, to make it go by more quickly?

But perhaps each of us can also recall experiences in our life that have felt more 'timeless', in the sense that time was not at all oppressive, but more open and plentiful? Maybe we had no sense of time at all, or were completely unconcerned by it, and could just forget it, in a way that felt free and liberating. Our sense of time can become flowing and deep, rich and abundant. It unfolds naturally and organically, it pours forth at its own pace, in its own rhythm. A few days can seem like a few weeks, can feel full, deep, and brimming. Time is no longer oppressive, but open and expansive. We are liberated from the prison of time. We experience 'free time'; we have glimpses of timelessness – moments of beauty, deep communication, creativity, meditation, or being absorbed in helping others – that seem to take us out of time altogether.

In other words, time is a state of mind. Time is not something we are *in*; it is something that we *are*. We and time are intimately intertwined. Our relationship with time therefore tells us something important about our relationship with ourselves. A particular state of mind is also a particular state of time. Our mental and emotional mood correlates with a certain mode of time. And that means we have a choice about our experience of time: what we do with our minds and our hearts, with our thoughts and emotions, will condition the quality of the time we live in.

Time-sense and the quality of our attention

Many of us love to travel because, when we arrive in a new country or culture, our senses and mind can be stimulated and enlivened. Even everyday objects or encounters become less ordinary because they are just slightly different from what we are accustomed to: the lamp posts are a quirky shape, the air has a distinctive aroma, or the crowds of people in the streets have a different energy. For the first few days, especially, everything is fresh, new, exciting. We discover new tastes each time we eat a meal. We hear what, to us, is a strange babble and sing-song of voices. The cut of clothes, the design of buildings, the colour of the blossom on the trees: everything is altered from what we are used to, and this heightens our awareness. Consequently our time can seem richer, thicker, fuller. Time stretches pleasantly. After only a few days, 'home' is a distant memory; we feel as though we have been away for weeks.

It can be the same when, for example, we start a new job, or embark on new studies at college. We find ourselves in a new environment making new friends and meeting new acquaintances, having new experiences, learning new skills. Our mind is fully activated, a greater attention is demanded of us, and we are charged up into a fuller awareness. Again, the days can seem like weeks, and the recent past is a faraway memory. Our sense of time shifts noticeably.

If you were to go on retreat for a week or two, it would involve living very simply, doing very little, talking less, having plenty of time and space between activities. So, in this case, there would be less stimulation in the quantitative sense. Yet the spaciousness of the retreat allows us to pay closer attention to our experience, so that there can actually be *more* happening in a qualitative sense. We observe and feel with greater than usual acuity and sensitivity the shifting and turning of our thoughts and moods. We enjoy the sunlight poking through the treetops and we notice birdsong that usually would pass unheard over our heads. We start to remember our dreams more vividly. We are able to be more mindful, and that means being more time-full. Time expands and unfolds.

Psychologists describe experiences of 'flow' that can occur when we are engaged in an activity that is completely absorbing.[3] If we are doing something that requires skill and concentration, and where we feel we have control over the task and receive immediate feedback on how well we are doing, then we may experience a deeply satisfying sense of flow. Our interest and attention are fully captured. We are totally focused. But we are not focused in a forced or strained way. It is not like knuckling down – with clenched jaw and furrowed brow – making ourselves complete an assignment because the deadline is looming, and not because we really want to do it. Instead, there is a naturally engaged, but also relaxed, focus and attention in which all our energies are flowing quite easily in one direction. Interestingly, one of the characteristics of flow is absence of time-sense. When we are 'in the flow', we forget about time.

There are other circumstances that can radically alter our attention and awareness and so change our time-sense. If we are involved in an accident, or we receive a sudden shock, our mind can go into hyper-alert. Our body urgently pumps itself with adrenaline, kicking our system wide awake, forcing all our resources and attention onto our immediate situation. People who have been in car crashes, for example, describe how time seems to slow dramatically, drastically decelerating. Suddenly everything is happening in sickening slow motion. They can be aware of thoughts and perceptions just as they rise up in the mind, moment by moment, and each one is separate and distinct. The mind's emergency survival instinct slows time right down; the mind generates experience at a different rate of time.

In brief, when we pay attention to our experience with a deeper quality of awareness, time expands and deepens. However, when our attention is forced or adrenaline-induced, time may still expand, but it won't deepen. We find ourselves instead in that weird bubble of slowed-down time.

And then, after the emergency has passed, our time-sense can rearrange around it. After a highly significant event, or being given a piece of news that had a big impact, we can often, even years later, still remember exactly where we were, what we were doing, even what we were thinking about, at the precise moment it happened. Time stands still, and then rearranges itself around that event. The mind takes the unusual occurrence as its reference point, makes it into the moment around which time stopped and started again. In the words of British nature writer Robert Macfarlane:

> [T]ime shivers and reconfigures itself about that moment, that incident. Everything leads up to it, or spirals out of it. Temporarily, you have a new centre of existence.[4]

Caring for loved ones who are seriously ill or dying can also take us out of our usual, habitual concerns and selves, which is to be taken out of our usual mode of time. In the presence of someone who is dying, our priorities rearrange themselves; perhaps we find ourselves dropping many of our everyday worries or preferences, in the flow of just attending to someone else's needs. We know there is not much time; each hour is precious, each day is special. Of course, circumstances vary; sometimes we are overtaken by fear or grief, but at other times, even if the situation is sad and painful, it can also be strangely rich and beautiful. Death summons us more fully into life and into the present. And this thickens the potent brew of time, makes it dense with emotion and meaning. Every moment has heightened significance.

By contrast, I might rush out of the house at the last minute, knowing I have 6 minutes to get to the station to catch the 7.23am train, which should get me into town at 7.57, so that I hopefully have time to pick up a coffee and still get into the office by quarter past, leaving me just about enough time to get the agenda ready for the meeting that starts at nine. I am intensely focused on clock time, but it is a heady, speedy mode of awareness that leaves no space for the fullness of my experience. If we are always rushing to meet the next deadline, then time rushes too. If the train runs late, then, very quickly, an immense pressure of time builds up. Frustration at being held up boils inside us. It may not be long before it reaches bursting point. Hurriedly preparing that agenda, we glance at our watch and can't understand where the time has gone: it seems to simultaneously speed up and dissolve down into nothing. There is never any time to spare; time is always running out.

The word 'boredom' is a relatively recent addition to our vocabulary, not found in dictionaries before the mid-eighteenth century. It seems plausible that the word 'boredom' could have been derived from the verb 'to bore', as in the 'boring' of a hole. Boredom is to go endlessly round and round the same old circle, stuck in an ever deepening rut; it is grindingly dull, blunting the keen edge of our awareness. The word 'tedium' is from the Latin *teadium*, 'to weary'; that which is tedious is mind-numbing, brain-deadening, sending us to sleep. It is time that is tiresome. Boredom is the dull, soporific, monotonous trudge of time. There is nothing that appeals to or attracts our attention, and so the temptation is to zone out, to distract ourselves, to try and make the time pass. But that only seems to make it drag by ever more slowly.

To be more aware is to be more alive, to have more life. It is to have more time, in the sense of a deeper and richer experience of time. Mindfulness is time-full-ness. If we live a truly mindful life, we will live longer! When we are aware and engaged, then our mind is both sharper and more sensitive; we experience more clearly and subtly. Conversely, when our interest is not activated, and our attention becomes more thin, wavering, and partial, then so does our experience of time. Time may go more slowly, as in the case of boredom, and that empty, hollow vacuum of time. Or time may flit by more quickly, as in the case of unmindfully rushing, but it seems a thin, insubstantial, and shadowy time that passes us by unawares. The kind of awareness and attention we bring to bear on our experience strongly flavours the quality of our time.

Human life stages and perceptions of time

Our subjective experience of time also varies through the different phases of our life. We all know how young children can be fascinated and enthralled by simple things, such as splashing around in rain puddles, or staring large-eyed at some cows in a field. Children can be intensely alive to things because, to them, they are so fresh and new. Watching children at play can provide a delightful, but maybe also poignant, reminder to adults of how they were once curious and entranced by the world. But now, whilst the children play for hours on end in the garden, the adults have fallen into the world of clock time. As soon as we come out of adolescence, time starts speeding up, as Billy Bragg once sang:

I was twenty-one years when I wrote this song,
I'm twenty-two now but I won't be for long...[5]

There are precious occasions – relaxing in natural beauty or contemplating art, perhaps – when adults can re-enter that more timeless world. As the French philosopher Frédéric Gros says of the pleasures of walking:

> having nothing to do but walk makes it possible to recover the pure sensation of being, to rediscover the simple joy of existing, the joy that permeates the whole of childhood [...] [walking] puts us in touch with that childhood eternity once again. I mean that walking is so to speak child's play.[6]

Obviously children do also enter the world of time. In the 1960s, a famous psychology experiment was conducted in which young children were given a marshmallow by an adult. Each child was told they could have another marshmallow in 5 minutes when the adult returned to the room, but only if they hadn't eaten the first one. The experiment was investigating what psychologists termed 'delayed gratification' – our ability to delay pleasure *now* for a greater pleasure *later*. On the internet you can find more recent replays of the experiment, in which hidden cameras film the children once the adult has left the room. Some of them sit on their hands and purse their lips, some of them tap their fingers on the table like anxious adults, and some stare longingly at the marshmallow with a vexed expression. Others engage in various displacement activities, singing or talking to themselves, or tapping their feet impatiently on the floor. One child even turned the sweet upside down, picked a little bit out of the bottom, popped this into his mouth, and then, just before the adult returned, turned the sweet the right way up again and pretended nothing was amiss. Evidently, for a child waiting for a second marshmallow, 5 minutes was an extremely long time.

Flexi time

In other words, time is calibrated differently for adults and children. To a three-year-old, adults seem incredibly old. Even getting to be aged four is an epic journey. In the course of the year from their third to their fourth birthday, a child lives through a third of their current span of life. For a fifty-year-old, however, one more year represents just another fiftieth of their life. I remember, as a young boy in the 1970s, lying awake in bed one night doing sums in my head. I calculated that when we reached the year 2000 I would be thirty-two years old. It seemed impossibly far away and hard to fathom. A couple of years ago I met the daughter of an old school friend of mine. I remembered her being born in the year 2000. Now, sitting chatting to her, I couldn't quite believe she was already sixteen years old, a delightful and friendly young adult. How had sixteen years passed by so quickly? Where had they gone?

Studies show that our perception of time does speed up as we grow older and as our metabolism slows. This may be partly due to the number of new experiences we are having. When we are very young, everything is different and new, and our minds are busy learning and storing memories. Once we are older, a lot of life is familiar, routine, and habitual; mostly we are just getting by, managing the days and weeks without much 'new' experience. This can make time seem more fleeting and quicksilver. When we're young, most of our life is in front of us, over the horizon. When we're older, most of our life is behind us, fading into the distance. Our short-term memory may fail, and the memories we are left with are from further back in our life. There are not so many pleasant experiences to look forward to, but quite possibly more unpleasant and uncertain ones. Consequently, there may be a natural shift through life from being more future focused to being more orientated to the past.

Time-sense, craving, and aversion

Samuel Beckett's *Waiting for Godot* is a play about waiting and, therefore, a play about time. Two tramps hang out by a roadside waiting for a mysterious character called Godot. They believe that, once they meet him, they will be saved. Until he comes, however, they can do nothing except wait. To pass the time, they talk, joke, argue, reminisce, do physical exercises, and fool around. Sometimes there are excruciatingly long silences when neither of them can think what to say. One begs the other to say something – anything – to fill that silence. Once, after a particularly good stretch of banter, one of them remarks joyfully to the other:

> Vladimir: That passed the time.
> Estragon: It would have passed in any case.
> Vladimir: Yes, but not so rapidly.[7]

Beckett's argument is that we can live our lives in anticipation of some (imaginary) future, and our lives (which are *now*, not in the future) are lived in suspense, on hold. We are not really living, merely waiting. The play has a quietly desperate, claustrophobic, almost unbearable sense of time, although it is also wickedly funny and very perceptive.

Let's move from a literary to a real-life example of an oppressive experience of time. Vidyamala is the founder of an organization called Breathworks that teaches mindfulness as a way of alleviating the suffering of people living with chronic pain.[8] As a child she damaged her back pulling someone out of a swimming pool, and a few years later it was made worse when she was involved in a serious car accident. The pain that followed in the next years was severe and exhausting. She found herself in hospital receiving specialist treatment and then, one night, needing to sit upright through the whole night to avoid possible complications to her wrecked spine. She was young, bright, and ambitious; her life and career had just been taking off. Now, all of a sudden, she was in hospital, alone, in agony, powerless to move or do anything. It was like being in hell. How could she possibly bear it? How could she possibly endure the night until the consultant came? Endless panicky thoughts, fears about the future, went on the rampage inside her mind. It felt like they were spinning her round and round, and dragging her down into madness. It was unbearable. She had no choice, however, but to bear it. How could she possibly get through the night?

This is how she describes what happened next:

Suddenly out of the chaos came something new. I felt a powerful clarity and a voice said, *"You don't have to get through until morning. You only have to get through the present moment."* Immediately, my experience was transformed. The tension torturing me opened into expansiveness as I realised the truth of what the voice was saying... that life can only unfold one moment at a time... that the present moment is always bearable [...] Fear drained out of me and I relaxed.[9]

It was completely understandable, given the severity of Vidyamala's situation, that she was pushing away the pain and in an extreme state of aversion to her experience. In such a state, however, the night felt intolerably long. Only once she was able to drop that fear and aversion and stay in the moment did time become less oppressive and more manageable. Her attitude to the pain and her sense of time were correlative.

This is a strong and dramatic story, but we all know more ordinary instances of the same phenomenon. I remember attending my first weekend retreat. I was young, terribly shy, and there were about sixty people on the retreat who all seemed to know each other, whilst I knew hardly anyone. On the second morning I found myself, along with everyone else, in the shrine room meditating. I was feeling out of my depth and out of place. I just wanted to run out of the room, grab my bag, and escape. But I was too shy and nervous to do that (and, in the long run, I am so glad I didn't). I longed for the bell to ring to finish the session. Instead, the silence stretched on and on. Those 50 minutes of meditation felt like 5 hours.

I once read a lovely story about a Zen master flying back home after a teaching trip to the USA.[10] One of his pupils had arranged his travel and was accompanying him to the airport, only the bus hadn't turned up and she was desperately worried about him missing his plane. In my mind's eye I can vividly imagine this scene, her pacing up and down the pavement, and looking at her watch every couple of minutes. Waiting, waiting, waiting. Cars and lorries roar past. Occasionally a bus does appear and she peers hopefully at the number on the front. None of the buses are going anywhere near the airport. Time lurches onwards at a frightening pace. There is a tight knot of tension and irritation growing in her stomach. Maybe she feels foolish for not aiming to catch an earlier bus. Perhaps she is worried about what other people will think if they hear that the teacher failed to arrive at the airport on time. She feels bad that he isn't experiencing a smooth and pleasant journey.

She looks over to the Zen master. He has placed his suitcase on the pavement and he is sitting on it, face turned to the sun, enjoying the glance of sunshine on skin. She realizes that he is not worried. Not only is he not worried, *he isn't even waiting*. He notices her looking at him and he turns and gives a reassuring smile. The twinkle in his eye contains just a hint of mischievousness, telling her not to worry either. It would be good if the bus turned up and he reached the airport on time. But his happiness doesn't depend on it; he hasn't staked his happiness on the future, on the contingent and uncontrollable. He won't exactly be happy about missing the plane, but it won't be the end of the world either.

He knows that to stake his happiness solely on the future is to start tying knots in the fabric of time, knots like the one rucked up inside her stomach. He doesn't tense and tighten, and so, for him, time doesn't tighten either. He doesn't kick against their predicament and so isn't boxed in by time.

So, looking more deeply into the elasticity of time, we see that *craving and aversion* also strongly condition our experience of time.[11] When we are craving for something in the present, or aversive to some anticipated future experience, this accelerates our experience of time. When we are trying to avoid our current experience, or longing for some future state, time seems to drag its feet. Perversely, time seems to do the opposite of what we want it to! Time flies when we are having fun. But a watched kettle never boils. Longing for the pain to end, or wanting the difficult meditation to be over, only made the experience of them seem longer. For those children waiting for a second marshmallow, a period of 5 minutes was a huge obstacle to overcome. If I am dreading an interview coming up this afternoon, or wanting more time to prepare for it, it seems to zoom up quicker. The woman waiting with the Zen master for the bus to the airport wanted more time now, and didn't want the future hour (when the plane was scheduled to depart) to come, but this, too, only seemed to bring it rushing onwards.

In other words, our ability or inability to be *with* our experience determines the sense of time in which we have the experience. To push against the present moment (aversion) elongates that moment, and so slows time. To grasp at the moment (craving) compresses it, and time passes more quickly. In this way, there is not just a psychological, but an ethical and karmic,[12] dimension to time. The thoughts and emotions, ethically either skilful or unskilful, that we generate in our minds will condition our experience of time, thereby creating the habitual modes of time that we live in.

Free Time!

To experience real contentment, the absence of craving and aversion, we need to forget about time. Imagine sitting in the garden on a sunny spring day. It has been a long, grey winter and today is the first really warm day of the year. It is so pleasurable to feel the glow of the sun on one's skin and to look up into that bright blue sky. Then a grey cloud strays into view. As we notice this cloud, a thought also drifts into our mind: we start wondering how long the sunshine will last. And this is the beginning of our discontent. Immediately there comes into our experience a subtle but nagging sense of tension. We find ourselves glancing up at the sky, worrying whether the cloud will obscure the sun. We reach for our phone to check the weather forecast. We are no longer enjoying the sunshine, at least not fully and unreservedly enjoying it. Deep down, we do know, of course, that the experience *can't* last. It is not in the nature of anything to last. Yet that doesn't stop us feeling disappointed and discontented. We try to hold on, even though we know that doing so is impossible. As the poet Louis MacNeice wrote:

> The sunlight on the garden
> Hardens and grows cold,
> We cannot cage the minute
> Within its nets of gold[13]

There can often be, threaded through our experience, this psychological and existential sense of imperfection, or incompletion – what the Buddha referred to as *dukkha*. To be truly content, we would need to be entirely equanimous about the sunshine. To enjoy the sunshine requires being free of needing the sunshine to carry on. Our happiness would not really depend on whether the sun shines or the sky clouds over. Contentment is the forgetting of time. As Buddhist teacher and writer Sangharakshita expresses it:

Lasting satisfaction is possible only outside time, where the question of its lasting does not arise.[14]

Or, to put it another way, in order to find lasting satisfaction, we have to drop the idea of it lasting.

Actually, I need to qualify what I said about contentment being the 'forgetting of time'. We do 'forget' in the sense that we cease being worried about how long the sun will shine. Nonetheless, simultaneously, we may also be aware of time. We might know, for example, that we have one hour in which we can enjoy sitting in the garden before we need to depart for work. But we can let go of thoughts of it being *only* one hour. In that hour we can feel we have all the time in the world. In order to feel that, however, we will need to drop craving and attachment.

Time as a commodity

So far we have explored how the quality of our attention influences the quality of our time. We have also looked at how aversion and craving, pushing away from and pulling towards experiences, rebelling against and welcoming them, also compress or elongate time. There is one last factor to consider in this chapter, and that is how our underlying *view* of time also determines our experience of it. This view may not be consciously held, or it may go in and out of conscious awareness. Nevertheless, we probably have certain ideas and assumptions about time that strongly influence our attitude to it, and that result in particular behaviours in respect of time. Most likely each of us has a certain 'working model' of what time is, and we tend to think and act automatically on the basis of that model. If the model is flawed, however, it will lead us into unhelpful behaviour patterns, and, consequently, into an oppressive and unsatisfactory experience of time.

Free Time!

We may habitually think of time as something external to us, something we exist *in*. We may not usually be aware of the relationship between our state of mind and our sense of time. Living in a society where 'clock time' is so all-pervasive most likely reinforces this view of time as something real, objective, linear, fixed, and external. (We will be looking at the history and culture of clock time more fully in the next chapter.)

This external view of time leads us into thinking of time as something we can *have*. We treat time like a possession, or a commodity: we can buy time or spend it, it can be saved or wasted, it can be invested, organized, and managed. Time becomes like a container into which we try to fit as much as possible. It is like booking onto an aeroplane flight on which we are only allowed one piece of baggage, so we stuff our suitcase to bursting point, and become red faced and slightly annoyed trying to force the zip shut.

Many of us will know the experience of having 10 minutes to spare before we need to leave the house. We get one more chore done, then we look at the news headlines online, then we think we will just quickly answer that email before we go. Before we know it, we are rushing out the house 10 minutes late instead of 10 minutes early. We're time greedy. We can't resist the temptation to pack more into any spare moments of time.

Occasionally I have a free day, a whole day off, stretching ahead of me. There is a novel I want to finish reading, I will go for a walk, I need to phone my brother, it would be good to do some gardening, and then I plan to cook a meal for a friend who is coming to visit. I want to do it all. I want to somehow squeeze everything in. And the time that felt so free and spacious starts to feel tight and constricted.

On a day off, to keep using that example, we might quickly and efficiently finish our household chores so that the rest of our day is free. It is not primarily the *speed* but the underlying *attitude* that determines the quality of our experience. It is not getting things done fast so we will have more time later that is the problem, but rushing at it in such a fashion that when 'later' comes we are too frazzled to enjoy the things we had been looking forward to. We end up fighting our way through what we have to do now, like hacking through a jungle. Every task, every incident, even the people we encounter, come to feel like obstacles. We have to get them out of the way, so we can get to the future. What we are engaged with now is just a hassle that we have to get through, and then our real life can begin again. And so we try to crash through our tasks and appointments as speedily as possible. But once we get to where our real life was supposed to resume, we are not in a fit state to live it. Like a clock that has been wound too tight, our mind can't stop its frenetic tick-ticking. The stuff that we smashed furiously aside still ricochets round the inside of our head. We feel like we have drunk a gallon of caffeine.

For some of us, this becomes a whole way of life. Our attitude to living is one of trying to get to the bottom of the 'to do' list. We imagine that, once we get there, *then* we can start really living. Our life isn't *then*, however. Our life is what is happening right *now*. A 'myth of completion' is propelling us, rather similarly to how some people are driven by an unhelpful 'myth of perfection'.

The poems of Jaan Kaplinski often consist of seemingly ordinary happenings, everyday observations, even, sometimes, just lists of commonplace objects, until the reader notices that there is something more significant that the poet is alluding to. One such poem lists jobs that need attending to: the leaking roof, the door that doesn't close properly, the children's clothes that need mending, the fence that, once repaired at one end, just collapses at the other:

The washing never gets done.
The furnace never gets heated.
Books never get read.

Life is never completed.
Life is like a ball which one must continually
catch and hit so that it won't fall.[15]

When we die there will still be messages in our email inbox. There will still be bills to pay. Just like the painting of the Forth Bridge, a job that is famously endless, the house maintenance will never be finished. It is only when we drop the idea that life can be completed that we are likely to find any sense of satisfaction and completion in getting tasks done.

Of course there is an objective aspect to time. We live in a world of change, and we do only have so much time. (The Zen master's plane *will* leave at a certain juncture.) We obviously can't treat time as entirely subjective, but nor are we separate from time. Time isn't something we can *get*, it is something we *are*. We explore this in more depth in chapter 9 of the book, but this view of time as separate from us is an aspect of our view that we have, or are, a self or ego separate from what is around us, apart and aloof from our experience of the world. We separate and reify our experience into me 'in here' and something 'out there', instead of seeing how they are mutually dependent. They don't exist separately, by themselves; rather, they arise interactively.

Our view of self as separate leads us into viewing time as separate from us. This deludes us into treating time like an external container. This container of time is divided off into sections; there is a section now that we want to fast-forward through as soon as possible, and a section later where we will stop so our real life can begin. But life doesn't work like that. It can't work like that because we and time are not divorced from one another, but intimately related and connected. We are joined at the hip.

2 o'clock

Clock time

We live in a world of clock time. Our lives are divided up into days, hours, and minutes. Clock time is everywhere; it is the organizing principle of virtually every aspect of our lives. Clocks, watches, and the more recent proliferation of mobile phones and electronic devices mean that clock time is never more than a glance away. It often has us physically surrounded. The oven in the kitchen, the phone in the hallway, the DVD player in the living room, the computer in the office: all sorts of appliances are on a default setting that constantly tells us the time. Listen to the radio and the presenter won't let us forget it. Watch breakfast TV and clock time stares at you from a corner of the screen.

To participate in our society is to take part in a social convention called clock time. Transport systems, offices and workplaces, the production and distribution of goods, public services, and retail: all run according to it. Even our leisure time is clock time: if you want to go to the cinema or book a table at a restaurant you are making use of it. Recently I ran a day workshop at a Buddhist centre on time and we ended with a period of meditation. Some people wanted to be sure it would end promptly; their cars were parked in the multistorey car park and their tickets ran out on the hour. Meditation needed to start and finish on the dot.

In a book entitled *In Praise of Slow*, Carl Honoré writes:

The clock is the operating system of modern capitalism, the thing that makes everything else possible – meetings, deadlines, contracts, manufacturing processes, schedules, transport, working shifts.[16]

Clock time is the essential facilitator and organizer of our complex society, and of all the choices and possibilities that we have come to expect. It enables everything, but does it also dominate everything? Captain Clock: is he a beneficent ruler, or a tyrannical dictator? Does he free up potential and possibility, or does he oppress our time and impinge upon our lives?

There is, in other words, a cultural, socio-economic, even political, aspect to time. In the previous chapter we looked at the psychological and ethical conditioning of time. But the way we experience time is also, at least in part, socially constructed. It is shaped and moulded by the time conventions of the society we live in. Clock time enables a society in which there is so much choice and possibility. It also conditions us into a particular idea and experience of time. It is instructive to consider this: if we want a more free and healthy relationship with time, then we need to reflect on how we relate to clock time. The next two chapters look at our cultural assumptions and beliefs about time.

Perhaps especially to those of us living in the 'developed world', clock time is so ubiquitous that it seems completely 'normal', self-evidently and obviously true and real. It is easy to forget how recent a phenomenon it is, or at least how recently it has become so pervasive and widespread. Whilst mechanical timekeeping devices have been around for nearly 1,000 years, it is only in the last 200 years or so that ordinary people have owned clocks and watches. Before that, only a more wealthy family would have owned a clock. It might have stood proudly in the hallway and been something of a status symbol. Or, in a European town or village, there might have been a clock face on the church tower.

Clock time

Early on, clocks only had an hour hand: the minute hand was a later development, and the hand showing seconds came later still.

Sundials were, of course, an early timekeeping device, around before mechanical clocks would have been common. A mechanical clock divides the day into twenty-four equal units of time. A sundial divides the *daylight* into twelve units. In regions of the world that lie far from the equator, there is less daylight in the winter and so, divided into twelve, this gives a shorter unit of time. In the summer, there is more daylight and the unit of time will be longer. In other words, an hour as defined by a sundial goes by faster in the winter and slower in the summer. The hours concertina: gradually growing longer from the winter to summer solstices, and then, from summer to winter, gradually getting shorter again. Sundial time has a closer relationship to the natural cycle of the days and seasons, the dance of the earth and the sun.

However, sundials don't work on a cloudy day, or during the night-time. In medieval Europe there were attempts to invent mechanical devices that marked out the same hours as sundials, but this was very difficult to achieve. The very nature of mechanical timekeeping devices is that they are *mechanical*: they operate using springs or pendulums that measure fixed, evenly spaced, units of time. 'Clockwork' is not like natural, 'organic' time, but keeps going, uniform, predictable, and regular, regardless of nature and season. Since it was much easier to produce devices that divided the day into uniform units of time, these were the clocks and watches that worked and were developed, and the kind of time that they measured became the accepted convention.

To some degree, therefore, our understanding and experience of time arise out of how we measure time: it is technologically determined. Humans have a desire to measure time. As a consequence, particular mechanical means for doing so come to the fore, and these then condition our notions and practices of time.

Past and different time-worlds

We have become completely used to mechanical clock time, but, not so long ago, people lived in a different time-world. Can we free ourselves of the assumptions and mindset of our contemporary world and try to imagine what this was like? What would people's relationship to time have been before clocks and watches became common personal possessions?

In Europe more than 200 years ago, we would have been much less likely to *see* the time on a clock face; we would most likely have *heard* it – a bell in the local church would have tolled the time. Time was heard and not seen. The church bell might have sounded every hour, or at most every quarter. In other words, the marking of time was more spaced out and occasional, the day was not so frequently divided up and structured by clock time. Time was less all-pervasive, less urgent; it passed more slowly. Time sounded in the distance, more of a backdrop in the life of a community. You listened out for the time, and, when the bell rang, you knew to prepare for church or to go inside for the curfew. Time was more in the background, but also more of a collective and communal experience. Time today, by contrast, is more ever present, but also a more private and individual experience.

In the early nineteenth century, the time in London could be slightly different from that in Cardiff or Edinburgh. Given the available means of communication and transport, it would have been very difficult to accurately synchronize time, and nor was it necessary. The growth of national railway networks, however, required timetables, and these necessitated standard time. It wasn't until 1855 that most of Britain accepted that Greenwich Mean Time was *the* time. Only in 1912 did an international conference agree a standard time across the world and the system of time zones. Trains and now planes needed to run on time, and that meant setting and standardizing time. Prior to this, time was more relative, more a *local* convention or custom, less precise, more approximate, not so uniform and universal.

Ten years ago I travelled to Malawi with my family. It was the first time I had visited a non-Western, non-industrialized country. The plane landed and taxied over to the airport building and the passengers emerged, blinking in the strong sunlight. On top of the airport building there was a sign that said 'waving platform'. This referred to the flat rooftop on which was a space where people could wait, either to wave goodbye to departing passengers, or to wave a welcome to a friend who had just arrived. The waving platform was about half full of people. Music played fairly gently through some loudspeakers. The people up there were sitting still and quiet. In the heat it did make good sense not to move around but to stay still and calm. Yet there was something else about the atmosphere that struck me, although I couldn't tell what it was straightaway. The people up on the platform simply sat, hands folded in their laps, or else shading their eyes as they tried to spot someone coming out of the plane, occasionally smiling and waving. But mostly they just sat, contained, sufficient, simply and patiently waiting.

We had flown (via Johannesburg) from Heathrow Airport where a plane took off at least every couple of minutes. At the airport in Malawi there might only be two planes landing on a given day. Heathrow was heaving with passengers on their way to their flights: rush and then queue to check in baggage, rush and then queue at security, rush and then queue to get through the terminal gate, rush and then queue to board the plane. Every minute a voice called on the tannoy: 'This is the final call for passenger Spate. Please proceed immediately to gate 38.' All along the vast corridors, shopping malls, and miles of chrome and glass, I felt that weird mixture of energies: anxious hurry and listless boredom.

Once on the plane, the flight attendants brought meals and drinks, keeping us distracted and occupied; they were like 'time managers', skilfully managing the boredom and discomfort of the long-haul flight. When the plane finally landed and came to a stop, almost all the passengers immediately switched on their phones and stood up, jostling into the central aisle, even though the doors weren't yet open. There was a build-up of restless energy.

Meanwhile, up on that waving platform, there was a tangibly different energy and atmosphere. Back then I wondered what it was and couldn't quite place my finger on it. Now I realize it was a different sense of time. Those people were waiting differently from the way I had ordinarily experienced waiting. Their waiting was more like that of the Zen master mentioned in the last chapter. They lived in a culture that still had a different notion of time. More and more of the world is becoming Westernized, but in some places you can, just about, still sense another kind of time. You can still witness and experience quite different customs and understandings of time. As Jay Griffiths observed when staying with tribal people living in remote rainforest:

> It happens when it happens: the doing of a thing and its timing are indivisible, the action is not jostled into the hour, but the hour becomes the action and the action becomes the hour. What to me was a distinction between the hour and the act was, to them, tautology, half artificial, half daft.[17]

Outside the airport, a Western tourist might ask what time the bus is leaving and be answered with a shrug, an uncomprehending look, and be told: 'It will leave when it is ready to leave.' The bus will depart only when it is full of passengers, or once the driver has finished his meal. It will be time to leave when the bus is *ready* to leave, rather than when the hands of a clock happen to be pointing in a certain direction. Time is not numbers on a clock. The Western tourist might be infuriated and exasperated, or they might give an amused, wry, knowing smile. But in that moment there is something interesting going on. We are witnessing a contrast to our super-efficient, but also super-anxious and super-driven way of living. We can see just how deeply we have changed our relationship with time. For sure, those peoples will have their own problems, hang-ups, and struggles; but in that contrast we see something about our particular Western way of doing time.

The Irish playwright John Millington Synge, who lived from 1871 to 1909, stayed for a while on the Arran Isles and wrote about his experiences and his observations of the lives of the islanders. It was like stepping back in time in many ways, including in respect of their attitudes to time. The islanders had heard of clocks, but nobody owned one, and their way of life meant they didn't really have a use for them:

> While I am walking [...] someone often comes to me to ask the time of day. Few of the people, however, are sufficiently used to modern time to understand in more than a vague way the convention of the hours, and when I tell them what o'clock it is by my watch they are not satisfied, and ask how long is left them before twilight.[18]

When the prevailing wind was northerly, the islanders kept the door on the south side of their houses open during the daytime. This let in the sunlight and so lit up the interior of the house. It also meant that the islanders could form an impression of the time of day by watching the shadow cast by the door. Where the shadow fell on the kitchen floor marked the passing of the day. If, however, the wind changed direction and came from the south, the islanders closed that door and opened up the one on the north side of their houses. This would still let in some daylight, but there would be no direct sunlight, and hence no shadow to tell the time. Synge had employed a local woman to cook him an evening meal each day. What time he received it depended on the direction of the wind. If her shadow-clock was in operation she would bring the meal around six. But if not, then he might get his evening meal in the mid-afternoon. Time was local, variable, and dependent on weather and season.

The shift to clock time

The social historian E.P. Thompson wrote an influential paper documenting the transition to clock time in eighteenth- and nineteenth-century Britain, relating it to the emerging industrialization of that era.[19] He argued that industrial capitalism necessitated new methods of incentivizing work, and hence new methods of payment. This required a new culture of time. In a pre-capitalist society, the seasons and rhythms of nature often determined what work was done and when. Farm labourers would work long and hard hours at harvest time, whilst in the winter they might have more leisure. A fisherman's work depended on the time of the tides and on the weather. Each day was organized much more by what needed to be done that day, and by the moods and cycles of nature. People's whole conception of time was different; it was 'task-orientated'. A job took as long as it took to get done.

Once workers were required to operate machines that ran continuously regardless of weather or season, the employer wanted to obtain the most possible out of their time. The employer might have paid their workers by the hour, or they might have paid them for every item they produced. Either way, the result is the same: 'Time is now currency: it is not passed but spent.'[20] Time becomes money.

In the pre-industrial economy, the work that got done was the work that needed to be done: the crop that needed to be harvested, the horse that needed to be shoed, or the milk that needed churning. 'Work' and 'life' were more intertwined. In an industrial culture, work became something that had to be done to earn a wage, and the worker was more distant and alienated from the need or purpose of the task. Working hours became more sharply demarcated from leisure time.

It was Benjamin Franklin who coined the phrase 'Time is money.' He went on to say: 'he that is prodigal of his Hours, is, in effect, a Squanderer of Money'.[21] There were different patterns across different industries, and there were cultural and national variations. (Thompson contrasts North America and Northern European countries where a Puritan work ethic held sway with, for example, Latin American countries where that ethic or cultural norm was not prevalent and where there remained a large proportion of the population living rurally and still in touch with the old ways.) Nevertheless, overall, the new working practices required a new ethic of time, a new moral value placed on punctuality, regularity, not wasting time but making the most productive use of it possible. Time now existed to be exploited.

'Time-orientation' took over people's lives, overthrowing and banishing 'task-orientation'. Their whole conception and experience of time was changed forever. The workers in the factories came to accept and internalize the new notion of time. Though they might have protested and struggled by striking for a better hourly rate, or for time-and-a-half for overtime, or for a shorter working week, they had, in effect,

> accepted the categories of their employers and learned to fight back within them. They had learned their lesson, that time is money, only too well.[22]

There have been critics of Thompson's theory[23] who argue that clock time was more prevalent before the Industrial Revolution and even before clocks and watches were commonplace. Such critics resist either technologically deterministic explanations of clock time (it was mechanical possibilities and inventions that made clock time happen) or socially deterministic accounts (clock time became all-pervasive once industrial capitalism required the synchronization of labour). They suggest that the differences between rural and urban time-sense have been exaggerated, and that pre-industrial rural people did understand and use clock time. They point out that clocks and other methods of timekeeping have been around for centuries, and social and cultural conventions of time therefore evolved much more gradually. They argue that it is absurd to think that something called 'clock time' suddenly started ticking away midway through the nineteenth century.

Of course it is easy to romanticize the past, to take a rosy view of what life was like before clocks and watches became ubiquitous. We do seem to perversely enjoy winding ourselves up about the evils of clock time, whilst forgetting all the choice, flexibility, and freedom it makes possible. Yet it seems hard to deny that our sense and experience of time have profoundly changed, as the account of Synge, or our own experience in non-Western cultures, testifies. Our idea of what time is, our beliefs about how we should be 'spending' time, and our consequent experience of it are socially and culturally conditioned and constructed. Timekeeping devices may have been around for many hundreds of years in big churches, universities, or wealthy houses. Yet that is not the same as a whole culture running on clock time. I find Thompson's account very persuasive. A majority of the world's population now lives in industrialized or post-industrialized towns and cities, more and more alienated from natural, organic cycles and seasons. The Protestant work ethic, in combination with a culture of wage labour, creates a new ethic of time. Humans advance in their power and ability to control the world to meet human desires, but each advance has a power *over* us too. Captain Clock rules our lives like never before.

Another huge and fundamental influence on our assumptions and beliefs about time is science. It was scientific advances that made industrialization possible, which then, as we've seen, fundamentally changed our ideas and behaviours in respect of time. But science itself was based on a new conception of time, which was integral to the Newtonian view of a mechanical universe that operated according to precise, predictable, and measurable mathematical laws. As the physicist Paul Davies explains:

> Newton plucked time right out of nature and gave it an abstract, independent existence, robbing it of its traditional connotations.[24]

He also quotes Newton's famous definition of time:

> absolute, true and mathematical time, [which] of itself, and from its own nature, flows equably without relation to anything external.[25]

Time was uniform, objective, and unaffected by anything else.

This Newtonian view of the universe, including its view of time, unravelled in the early twentieth century when Einstein published his theory of relativity, according to which time goes faster or slower depending on the motion of the person observing. And this is not just a theory; there is experimental evidence that confirms Einstein's predictions about the varying rate of time. Scientific ideas about the nature of time are still evolving. In an even more recent theory, known as 'quantum gravity', which aims to integrate relativity with quantum mechanics, things change and affect each other, but there is no underlying passage of time.[26] Whilst scientific ideas about time have changed radically, our conventional, everyday understanding of time still derives from the work of Newton in the late seventeenth century. The mechanical, Newtonian view of time imagined as a straight and uniform line along which we travel seems to have stuck in our minds, and remains the 'commonsense' view of time.

How real is clock time?

One theory about why *Homo sapiens* became dominant as a species on our planet is that we, even more than other human species, developed the cognitive skills to create cultures – shared understandings and practices that enabled large numbers of peoples, and even diverse groups of different tribes and nations, to cooperate and work together. Such a shared understanding only works if those participating in it trust it; they believe it to be real and true. A shared culture, something imagined and created by humans, becomes their reality.[27]

Clock time is one such cultural construct – a collective understanding and practice that has now become global. But we can forget it is just a human creation, a social convention. Clock time becomes so pervasive that it comes to be seen as entirely natural, normal, and real. We can no longer remember that there are other ways of being, other ways of doing time. It becomes very difficult for us to imagine how time might be experienced differently. Our view of time comes into focus through a very particular set of lenses, but we've been wearing these glasses all our life and we've become completely used to them. We've even forgotten we have them on. As Carl Jung once said: 'It is hard to see the lion that has eaten you.'[28]

In the Buddhist tradition is a list of ten 'fetters', deeply engrained mental and emotional habits that need to be broken in order to progress towards Enlightenment. The third of these fetters is 'rites and rituals as ends in themselves'. Perhaps the Buddha emphasized this because there was a lot of empty ritual, superstition, or ethical and religious formalism in the culture of his day. Ritual can be powerful and meaningful, tapping into something deep about being human, but only if we have engaged our hearts and minds and are truly open to change. Merely going through the motions, dutifully reciting the correct words, isn't, on its own, going to have a transformative effect. This third fetter is a kind of literalism; the outward sign or expression is mistaken for the inner process itself.

This idea can be applied to non-religious customs and conventions. They, too, can become 'ends in themselves'. We literalize them; they become such deeply embedded assumptions about how life works that they seem absolutely real, taking on a life of their own. Perhaps the culture of clock time can become a fetter in this way, can be a rite or a ritual that becomes an end in itself. We forget that, whilst clock time is a useful tool, a helpful cultural practice for organizing and coordinating our lives, it is not really what time is. Clockwork, mechanical time, is a way of measuring time, but it is not time itself.

Sometimes I go on 'solitary retreats'; I spend a week or longer somewhere in natural surroundings living quietly and alone. This has the effect of throwing me back on my own resources. It also shows me very strongly who I am. There is just me and so I can't blame my moods or feelings on anyone else. My own mind is all I've brought along with me, and I begin to see how much of my experience is created in my own mind, a product of my own habitual ways of perceiving and interpreting the world. This is a valuable and potentially very liberating lesson because, once we see what we do with our mind, we can start to exercise choice and make changes.

Solitary retreats are also very interesting and revealing with respect to our relationship to time. Whilst on a solitary retreat, I often hide my watch away so as to be free of clock time for a while, and to live in a more natural and spontaneous time, eating when I am hungry, sleeping when I am tired. To quote Henry David Thoreau:

It matters not what the clocks say or the attitude and labours of men. Morning is when I am awake and there is a dawn in me.[29]

Even so, it can be surprisingly tempting to dig that watch from the bottom of my travel bag and take a peek. Maybe I have just meditated and I want to know how long I meditated for, as if that tells me something about whether the meditation was 'good' or 'bad'. We have become so used to locating ourselves in clock time, justifying and measuring what we do by the clock's criterion. Time has become part of our identity. Clock time, in other words, provides an existential security or, rather, it temporarily covers up our insecurity.[30] It is valuable and fascinating finding these opportunities to explore our reliance on, or even addiction to, clock time, and to start to loosen up to it. We can learn to use clock time, but not be used by it. We don't have to run every aspect of our lives by clockwork, so that its mentality starts to take us over. (The final chapter offers some practical suggestions for *how* to do this.)

Clock time can subtly condition us into a more artificial and abstract idea of time, one that is linear, regular, and objective. This may reinforce the tendency to see time as a commodity that we must use, save, spend, manage, exploit, before it ticks away into oblivion. We can easily forget that all this is just metaphor. Were humans made for the hour, or were hours made for humans? We squeeze our life into the hour, measuring and defining everything by the clock. Our lives become far more clockwork than they need to.

3 o'clock

Tomorrow time

Around 10,000 years ago *Homo sapiens* made a gradual transition from a nomadic, hunter-gatherer life to living in more permanent settlements and growing crops and domesticating animals. Humans developed agriculture. From somewhere in my upbringing I had imbibed the view or assumption that this was a great leap forward for humanity, allowing us to live safer, more stable and secure lives, to become more civilized. Recently, however, I've read accounts that give a very different picture.[31] Admittedly, there is precious little hard evidence surviving from so long ago, but some clues have been found: by examining remains of human bones and artefacts, researchers are able to piece together theories about what human life might have been like in times before recorded history.

The hunter-gatherer life could be a good one. Provided you survived childhood, and provided you did not succumb to disease or suffer a bad accident, you could expect to live a long and healthy life. Adaptability and resourcefulness were the keys to survival, so ancient hunter-gatherers were very skilled and knowledgeable people. They would have acquired an intimate knowledge of what grew and lived for miles around them, and they moved from place to place, season to season. There was plenty of leisure time: time when there was nothing to do and nothing to worry about.

41

Although agriculture enabled more food to be produced, which allowed an expanding population to be sustained, the quality of life for the average individual became poorer during the age of agriculture. Evidence from skeleton and bone remains shows many physical ailments, particularly back injuries, stemmed from when humans began digging and working the land. Disease became more common because humans now lived close together in settled villages. The diet was less varied and was dependent on the success of just a few crops. Although the human population grew dramatically, individual life expectancy was shorter.

Undoubtedly the development of agricultural society also changed the human experience of time. A farming community always needs to plan ahead. Crops must be grown in spring to feed the animals through the next winter. Land must be prepared in winter for sowing, so that the field can be harvested next autumn. The success or failure of these enterprises, in which that community has invested so much time and energy, and upon which rests their survival, depends on factors beyond their control: weather, wild animals, or diseases and insects ruining the plants they have tended. This must have made for anxiety. Human beings would have become more *future-orientated*, and therefore more anxious. Their well-being now depended on an unknown future, and this necessitated more planning, anticipating, and being constantly on the lookout. In trying to exercise increased control over their fate, humans ended up much more under the thumb of time. Trying to control their destiny meant being ruled by the dictates of the future. While it's easy to idealize the hunter-gatherer life, nonetheless, in all likelihood those people were more able to live in the present. In an agricultural society, the point, the main purpose, of what you do today lies months, even years, ahead. You live much more in, and for, the future.

How and why did this shift to agriculture happen? We don't really know. One theory is that the hunter-gatherers themselves became too successful. They became adept at catching and killing large numbers of big mammals, and the human population increased. This created a pressure to sustain the burgeoning population, whilst wild animal populations were dwindling due to overhunting. So, although the transition to agriculture must have profoundly changed human experience, it is not necessarily the case that human nature was completely different before that transition.

We human beings have evolved and developed *self*-consciousness. We don't just have *sense*-consciousness; we can also be aware of having our sense experience, we can be aware of being aware. This enables us to 'stand back' from our experience, to observe and reflect. And, in turn, this allows us to understand our environment, to form ideas and theories about how it works, and then to set about trying to control and manipulate that environment to our own advantage. Out of this arises the whole human world, from the first primitive tools and artefacts, through to our modern world of science, culture, and astonishing human ingenuity, creativity, and sophistication.

Self-consciousness has huge advantages in terms of the human ability to adapt the physical world to meet our needs and desires. But there is a price. That human faculty of standing back, reflecting and understanding, and then envisaging how things could be different also helps create a distinctively human sense of restlessness and anxiety. However much we have, we can imagine, and then crave, having *more*, or *better*. However well things are going, we can imagine, and then feel aversion to, circumstances in which they might not go so well, so that we forfeit what we've earnt.

Human self-consciousness is a double-edged sword. It allows us to stand back, observe, understand, and control the world. Yet, in doing so, it creates that particularly human sense of dissatisfaction, that underlying, nagging feeling that we've never arrived, never finished, that no matter how busy we are or how much we get done, our life is never completed. In this chapter we are going to explore the kind of culture, and particularly the 'style' of time, that this future-orientation has created.

The flow of time in modern life

Look through lifestyle magazines, count the numbers of people enrolling in mindfulness stress-reduction courses, or listen to conversations in the office: there is a widespread perception that life in the twenty-first century is becoming relentlessly busier and faster, and that there is increasingly more pressure on our time. There is a growing area of research into 'time use' that has, in part, focused on this perception. Do we really have less time, or is it just a story we tell ourselves?

Research seems to indicate that, over the last decades in the USA and Europe, work time has actually decreased and leisure time increased. Even in recent years since the financial crash of 2008 and global recession, data from the American Time Use Survey (ATUS) shows no change in leisure time between 2004 and 2014, and no change in the average hours worked per day.[32] So why is there a perception of *more* busyness? The topic needs closer examination. Measuring hours spent on different activities may be too simple and crude an indicator; what is needed is a *qualitative* as well as quantitative assessment of our time use. I'm going to suggest two factors that may impact on the quality, the feel and texture, of our time. Firstly, is how we spend our time becoming more fragmented and bitty, pulling us in different directions, meaning the flow of our time gets yanked apart? Secondly, does living in a fast-changing society create a sensation of constant acceleration and make time feel like it is lurching forwards faster and faster?

Unquestionably the last twenty years have seen a huge technological revolution take place as a result of the internet.

There has been the rise of email, social networking, and instant downloading and access to film and music. These days millions of people carry an extension of their brain in the palms of their hands; it's via this 'smartphone' that we organize and conduct much of our lives. This new technology means that we can still respond to work emails when we are at home. Whilst we are out for a walk the phone can ring, we see it's a work colleague, and we answer the call. Perhaps we never really put our work down, never really 'switch off'. Then, whilst at work, we can carry on with our non-work lives, checking in on social media to see what our friends are doing, or going online to find out the weather forecast for the weekend. We can also multitask: whilst we wait on hold at the telephone call centre, we stare at the computer screen and the spreadsheet we are working on, whilst occasionally switching our attention to check if there are any messages on our mobile phone.

In all these ways and more, digital technology and personal devices give flexibility and adaptability. Yet they also mean that we're likely to pay attention to things in smaller, quicker chunks of time, and that our attention is more often pulled hither and thither, yanked that way by the bleep that signals an incoming text message, lured this way by the 'customers-who-bought-this-product-also-viewed' message on our screen. Technology is fast and efficient, but it also speeds up and short-circuits the flow of time. As we discussed in chapter 1, the quality of our awareness and attention profoundly influences the quality of our time. If our attention is bitty and fragmented, then our hours and days become bitty and fragmented too. Time froths and fizzes; it fidgets rather than flows.

I remember when mobile phones first became common. This occurred during a phase of my life when I was regularly leading group retreats and I could observe what happened. Once upon a time, in the days before mobile phones, people just came on retreat and were able to leave their daily life behind them. But once mobile phones became ubiquitous, people arrived on retreat and needed to phone home to let their family know they'd arrived. Then they phoned back 15 minutes later to remind them to feed the cat. Then they phoned the office to say they would deal with that query on Monday, and then they worried about the possibility of an emergency and about the mobile-phone signal being too weak in the countryside for a message to get through. It seemed to me that, as well as allowing ease of communication, mobile-phone technology also allowed a whole load of fussing and fretting, a mass of anxiety *that simply wasn't possible before*.

We tend to think technology gives us freedom and flexibility. And in some ways it does. Yet, simultaneously, it can trap and confine us. For example, I know self-employed people who say they cannot go on retreat without checking their phone every day, as these days their customers expect an instantaneous reply. Once upon a time these people were able to forget about their business for a few days and be on retreat carefree. Now they are in danger of becoming slaves to their work lives. Yes, technology gives us power. But it also has power over us.

A domestic appliance such as a washing machine saves us from dull and dreary labour. It saves time and yet it also fractures time.[33] We load up the machine, then start cooking dinner, we come back and unload the clothes and put them in the dryer, then we make a few phone calls, then we suddenly remember the washing again and rush back downstairs to unload the dryer and fold up the clothes. The washing machine and clothes dryer are convenient, allowing us to save time and get on with more important or enjoyable tasks. 'Convenience' is a sense of control over our lives and our time that we now take for granted, and that has become normal and habitual. We are hardly aware of what we are doing, how we are constantly organizing and time-managing our hours and days; the dynamics of our relationship with time are largely unconscious. We don't notice how much of our life is based around 'saving time'. We are constantly future-orientated, saving time now so that we feel we have more of it later.

Modern life has become more sophisticated or more complicated, depending on which way you look at it. There are more choices, more possibilities, and that entails more to organize, more details and appointments to remember. And that can mean more juggling, and that means more thinking, and that makes us feel even busier. We can become stuck in a loop: there are more things we want to do with our time, so we try to cram in as many of them as possible. This means that, even if the statistics and research tell us we have more leisure time, we don't believe it. We can *feel* we actually have less time, because the time we have is lower in quality. It feels more manic. We may be materially rich, but we feel time-poor.

The age of acceleration

In the early 1970s Alvin Toffler wrote a bestselling book called *Future Shock*.[34] His thesis was that:

> Change is avalanching upon our heads and most people are grotesquely unprepared to cope with it.[35]

'Future shock' was the culture shock of living in an era of accelerating and ceaseless change, of the dizzying and disorientating non-stop roller-coaster of late-twentieth-century life and culture. Toffler researched his book during the late 1960s, which was no doubt an era of huge and significant social change, and his book touched a nerve when it was published.

In hindsight, some of Toffler's claims seem overblown:

> As the rate of change in society speeds up, more and more older people feel the difference keenly. They [...] become drop-outs, withdrawing into a private environment, cutting off as many contacts as possible with the fast-moving outside

world, and, finally, vegetating till death. We may never solve the psychological problems of the aged until we find the means – through biochemistry or re-education – to alter their time sense, or to provide structured enclaves for them in which the pace of life is controlled, and even, perhaps, regulated according to a 'sliding scale' calendar that reflects their own subjective perception of time.[36]

Our experience of time does vary from childhood, through adulthood, and into old age. Yet human beings are often much more adaptable to change than we think or expect, including older human beings. I am sure we all know people in their seventies or eighties who enjoy learning, experimenting, and who are open to new experiences. The quote might even sound rather sinister, seeming to imply that it is those who resist change who have the problem and who may need, through medical or educational means, to be temporally regulated and readjusted. Whereas, in a traditional culture, the elderly are worthy of respect because they have the wisdom of age and experience, in the accelerating world, can the old be seen as has-beens, out of date, stuck in a time warp?

Nevertheless, despite some reservations about the tenor of the book, Toffler fascinatingly catalogues many of the ways our lives have changed, provides a wealth of data on just how profound and rapid these changes have been, and considers how all this, amongst other things, changes our sense of time. I am going to re-present some of his findings, in some cases with more up-to-date statistics.

Scientists believe that it was around 40,000–50,000 years ago that *Homo sapiens* began showing behaviours and cognitive traits that marked our emergence as a distinctive human species, and our gradual dominance over other types of humans. If we imagine roughly 50,000 years of *Homo sapiens* history as a single day, then timekeeping devices only enter the story in the last half-hour of the day. The widespread use and ownership of clocks and watches only started 6 minutes ago; for the first 23 hours and 54 minutes of the human day, the huge majority of humans did not own the means of telling the time.

For the first 23 hours and 45 minutes of that human day, there was no printing, whilst in the last 3 minutes we have seen the emergence of cinema, and then radio and TV. Computers have been widespread for less than a minute; the internet emerged within the last 30 seconds. We now have access to a wealth of information and culture from all over the world. TV channels provide non-stop up-to-the-minute news, live footage, and instant analysis. In that increasingly globalized and interconnected world the flow of information is faster, the issues more huge and complex, and it becomes harder to keep abreast of developments.

For 23 hours and 56 minutes of the human day, we could travel no faster than a galloping horse would carry us. We have had just 4 minutes in the day during which faster travel has been possible, and only in the last minute or so has air travel across the globe been affordable (at least for those in affluent societies). When the first migrants from Europe travelled to Australia or New Zealand, they set off on a sea voyage of several months. They said goodbye to family and friends and would never have expected to see them again. The journeys involved were just too long, expensive, and dangerous: to emigrate was to say goodbye forever. Nowadays we can fly round the world in a day or two, and we can hear or see each other, with just a split-second time delay, via telephone networks, the internet, and satellites orbiting the earth.

In 1850 there were four cities in the world with a population of over 1 million.[37] One hundred years later there were eighty-three and now, just sixty-five years after that, there are nearly 500.[38] Throughout the whole history of humanity, the vast majority of us have lived in wild or rural environments. In 1800, only 3 per cent of the world's population lived in cities; 200 years later the figure is nearly 50 per cent.[39] Soon, for the first time in human history, most of us will be urban dwellers. We have become creatures of human-built, densely packed, and fast-moving city environments.

In 2010 the human race used roughly twenty-six times more energy than in 1820. Taking into account population increases, each person was using an average of four times more energy per year, with the fastest increase taking place from the end of the Second World War until about 1970.[40] A hugely disproportionate amount of this increased energy use will have been in the affluent 'developed world' and, more latterly, in fast-growing economies such as China and India. This growth in energy use means that, in the last century, the human race has consumed as much energy as was consumed in all of the preceding 2,000 years.[41]

The amount of waste produced per person is rising.[42] A disposable drink bottle, for example, was unknown before the 1960s; we managed to stay hydrated without them. Yet plastic bottles now litter beaches and fill landfill sites the world over. Plastic waste in the sea is an extremely serious environmental issue. The human race produces about 1 million plastic bottles *every minute*, and it is predicted this will rise by 20 per cent by 2021 as a Western, urbanized, 'on the go' culture spreads to China and the Asia Pacific region.[43] We have become accustomed to a way of life in which we may buy and own a human-made object for no more than a few minutes, consuming its contents, and then simply throwing it away and forgetting all about it.

We have also come to accept a world in which the goods we buy are out of date or out of fashion within, at most, a few years; we are encouraged to purchase new, better, faster, smarter. Disposal of broken or superseded phones, computers, and electronic devices has become another huge environmental problem, creating tens of millions of tons of highly toxic waste every year. Much of it is shipped out to developing countries where environmental and health controls are non-existent, or at least less stringent, and where workers earn a few dollars a day salvaging traces of the precious metals and minerals that make up the circuit boards. In these and many other ways, there is a direct relationship between our modern desire to 'save time' and our despoiling of the planet.

Clothes, gadgets, furniture: the economies of mass production mean it is cheaper to buy new rather than get something fixed. Manufacturers also design goods so that they are replaced rather than repaired. I once owned some loudspeakers, and one of them developed a crackle that I knew was due to a loose connection. I could have easily fixed it, except that it had been built as a sealed unit. It simply was not possible to open it up and access the wiring; from the manufacturer's point of view, I was meant to throw it away and buy a new one.

In the times before recorded history, the basic conditions of human life would have remained the same for tens of thousands of years. For much of our history since then, the way people lived stayed roughly the same from one century to the next. In the last two centuries, however, the world we live in has changed from generation to generation. And now, in the last twenty to forty years, the rate of social, geopolitical, technological, and economic change has not slackened, or even plateaued, but, arguably, grown more rapid and more global, interconnected, and complex. Rapid acceleration can feel exciting and release a rush of adrenaline. But if it goes on for too long it can become frightening, disorientating, and lead to burnout. Ours is a world that is accelerating on multiple fronts simultaneously: through globalization, the revolution in information technology, and seismic ecological change. All this can make it seem as if time is going faster. Our sense of time – of the very fabric of human experience – is more frayed and fragmented, making us feel more frayed and fragmented, and sometimes more fractious too.

Time, money, and status

When time is money, it tends to be those who are cash-rich who feel time-poor. There is evidence that, in the USA and many European countries, it is the high-earning professionals who are working longer hours, in contrast to a trend towards more leisure time in the wider society. Leisure time amongst the highest earners increased in the 1980s but has more recently fallen back to 1960s levels again. Housing, pension, and education costs have risen, increasing the cost of high standards of living. There is more competition for good and interesting jobs. People want to spend more time with their children because they have high ideals and expectations about family life and what their children should be able to do and achieve. Those in the higher strata of society may feel time-pressured as never before.

Experiences of being time-poor are commonly based on the view, or belief, that more money equals more consumption, which equals more happiness. The first two parts of this equation (more money and more consumption) require more time: work hard, play hard. But, if we need more time to earn *and* more time for leisure, then the equation can never balance.

By contrast, many manufacturing and production-line jobs have disappeared from Western economies and moved to other countries with cheaper labour. Lower-paid jobs in Western societies tend to be in the service economy, to be low-paid, and low-skill, and, in recent years, wages have been stagnant. Many jobs are part-time, many on temporary or zero-hour contracts. There is higher unemployment. This means there are large numbers of people who may be time-rich, but they are cash-poor. They have time on their hands, but they may not know what to do with it, or have many resources with which to spend their time. Or they may be juggling two part-time jobs with raising a family. Their quality of time (and of life) will be different from that of a well-paid professional. They may not experience themselves so much as 'busy', but rather as being in stressful jobs without prospects, struggling to cope and make ends meet. They might have more 'spare' time, but its quality may be poorer.

Much of the literature and discussion on busyness and on the stresses of modern living, and that of the whole mindfulness industry, tends to focus more on the lifestyle of relatively well-off professionals and their stereotypically busy lives. However, whilst such people may feel stretched and long for 'quality time', for someone in low-paid work the issues may be different. In the nineteenth century, factory workers fought for increased leisure time and for better rewards for time spent on the production line. Today the politics of time are different. There are new social and economic factors that strongly influence the quantity and quality of our time.

Sometimes, secretly, we actually *like* to be busy; it's a sign of status. I remember, as a young man in a new job, making an appointment with someone who saw how empty my diary was, and remarked on this. The pages of my diary were mostly full of blank white spaces that symbolized unallocated time. Rather than being pleased, I was embarrassed. A full diary would show how busy I was, and therefore how important and indispensable. As the commentator and columnist Tim Kreider writes:

> Busyness serves as a kind of existential reassurance, a hedge against emptiness; obviously your life cannot possibly be silly or trivial or meaningless if you are so busy, completely booked, in demand every hour of the day [...] I can't help but wonder whether all this histrionic exhaustion isn't a way of covering up the fact that most of what we do doesn't matter.[44]

Modern world, modern time

The preceding chapter considers how the culture of clock time, which is a human creation, can become an end in itself. We can tend to forget that clock time is just a social construct and become conditioned into an underlying, subconscious idea of time as like clockwork: uniform, linear, regular, and objectively real. We constantly measure and calibrate time, and this reinforces our belief in time as a fixed resource, out of which we try to squeeze as much as possible. It makes it harder for us to see how time has an inner dimension, that our experience of time is determined by our attitude and how we relate to it. The result may be a vicious circle, as Buddhist writers David Loy and Linda Goodhew suggest:

> The more we experience time as objective, the more alienated is the sense of self that is *in* time and therefore more desperate to *use* time in order to try and gain something from it.[45]

This chapter focuses on how that culture of clock time is relentlessly future-orientated. Much of our 'Western' lifestyle, our technology, and our fast, throwaway, consumer culture is designed to 'save' time, so that we can get to our desired future, and get there quicker. Today, many of us can live longer and healthier, more comfortable and affluent lives than those of previous generations, yet there is a price. We can feel we have no time for really living; there is a hidden cost in terms of the inner quality of our time.

We have taken a broad sweep through many complex issues in the last couple of chapters. Our experience of time is socially conditioned, perhaps far more profoundly than we usually realize. Religiously and psychologically (the Protestant work ethic and individualism), economically and politically (industrialization and time becoming money), culturally (consumerism and our expectation of choice and convenience), scientifically (the Newtonian view of the universe), and technologically (mechanical timekeeping devices and electronic devices): in all these overlapping ways we are conditioned into a very particular mode of time. This conditioning adds up to deeply embedded assumptions and beliefs about what time is. An intrinsic part of the modern mind is a 'modern time' – a particular style of time, a way of doing time that is entrenched in the modern psyche. Clock time is fundamental to a whole worldview about what human life is, and how our time should be utilized. Clocks and timekeeping devices don't just tell us the time; in a subtle but fundamental way, they are telling us what time *is*.

Part II

Perspectives and practices on time

The photograph

After a school reunion, some of my old classmates post photos on the internet, snapshots taken in the early 1980s of my year group at school. I browse through them. I come across a photo of a red-haired girl with a big cheeky smile. Immediately a flood of memories surges into consciousness.

Suddenly I'm standing opposite Becca in the schoolyard. She's funny, sparky, bright, and outspoken. She talks loudly with a south London accent.

We're the same age, but she's taller than me. I feel awkward and shy. Wanting to be liked, wanting to be appreciated.

I like the teasing jokes she tells, how she shrieks with laughter, and the way she throws her arms up as she laughs, as if to push me away. This brings out the playfulness in me; it gives me permission to clown about, to tease her back. Will she like it, or will she be offended? Now I feel unsure again.

Intense, youthful desire to be loved surges through my body, mingled with anxiety and uncertainty. I watch the expression on her smiling face, the rosy glow in her cheeks, the sparkle in her blue eyes. I can just about smell her perfume.

Right now: what's the story?

Am I a fourteen-year-old larking about in the school playground?

Am I a forty-year-old looking at a photo of an old girlfriend?

Am I both?

Or am I something else again?

I chance upon a colour-faded photo and Becca flashes back into my life. I don't just remember the past: I *feel* fourteen again. Those feelings: where do they come from? To what time do they belong?

4 o'clock

Story time

Recently I revisited the area of south-east London where I grew up. I parked my car and walked along old familiar streets towards my childhood home. There was the same red postbox on the corner, and the windows and door of the house opposite were still painted the same shade of dark green as thirty years ago. If you had asked me in advance what the colour was, I could not have told you. I would not have been able to deliberately recall it. Yet as soon as I saw it, there was a feeling of recognition and familiarity. I *knew* it was the colour it had always been.

I noticed other very ordinary details – the shape of the lamp posts, the row of three bungalows, even the size and shape of the grass verges – that were utterly familiar. Suddenly it felt like only yesterday that I was a child walking along that street on my way to and from school. As I walked along, familiar objects came into view, and they just 'fell into place'; they felt somehow 'right'. This slotting into place was an experience of the external world, and also, at the same time, internal. I felt strangely familiar feelings and emotions too, feelings I had not felt for thirty years.

Then I passed our neighbour's house and came to the place where my childhood home should have been. The house was not there. My heart missed a beat; my whole nervous system gave a start. The house was not there! I experienced quite a shock. Sure enough, there was a building standing where my home had been. But it wasn't the house that I had lived in. I stared at it in dismay and disbelief.

After what seemed like a long time of standing and staring, I realized, with another shock, that it *was* my house. It had been modernized and modified almost beyond recognition. The whole building was rendered and painted, so I could no longer see the brickwork. The windows had been replaced with modern PVC double glazing. The front garden had been completely relandscaped and replanted. Now, as I looked at it, it was obvious that it was my old home, but for at least a few seconds I simply had not been able to see it. What I had *expected* to see was not there, and that had made it very difficult to take in what *was* actually there right in front of me. What my eyes took in hadn't matched my memory and that mismatch had, for a few moments, confused and confounded my faculty of perception.

Psychologists explain that our minds form 'interpretive frameworks' or 'working models'; we learn about an environment and our mind lays down memories, forming inner mental pictures or maps. Then, when we encounter that environment again (or a similar environment), those pictures or maps are ready to hand.

This chapter explores the nature of the past and the future, and our relationship to them. It argues that yesterday and tomorrow don't exist, except as inventions in our minds.[46] The past and future are also 'interpretive frameworks' or 'working models'. We explain to ourselves how we got to where we are now: that's the past. We predict and anticipate where things are going next: that's the future. Both are stories that we have told ourselves. But there are different kinds of stories: stories that are limiting and stories that are liberating. The way we talk to ourselves about our past and future, the type of thinking, interpreting, and 'modelling' that we engage in, is a crucial determinant of the quality of our lives.

Interpretive frameworks

As the example above shows, what we see, hear, or smell isn't based just on the sensory information taken in through our eyes, ears, or nose right there and then. It is also based on memories and associations and those inner frameworks. Memory, conscious or unconscious, conditions our perception in the present. A huge amount of interpretation and comparison takes place in our moment-by-moment construction of experience. (Perhaps this is why it can be so tiring to be in a new and unknown environment such as an unfamiliar city or a foreign country. Our mind has to make an intense effort, firstly to negotiate that situation with less help from its own internal working models, and secondly to begin mapping out new models.)

Our everyday experience of what we think is an objective and external world is not so purely objective and external. It is the mind's fabrication. Neuroscientists can observe and study the activity along different neural pathways as humans are engaged in different activities. The process of visual perception involves six times more activity between different areas of the brain's cortex than between the cortex and the thalamus (the part of the brain to which information from the eyes first travels). In other words, only a relatively small fraction of the information that forms a visual perception comes from the eyes. By far the biggest portion comes from other parts of the brain. Our eyes move four times per second, jumping about gathering in more information. We blink every few seconds, and each time we blink our eyelid is closed for 80 milliseconds. But we don't see a jumping about, flickering world; what we perceive appears stable and consistent. We don't see what our eyes see; we see an image constructed in the mind.[47] This image is made partly from information from the retina, and then from a whole host of other bits of information in the mind.

Usually these frameworks serve us well. We successfully manage our lives and complex situations. Someone walks past my window towards my front door; from just a split-second glimpse my mind effortlessly recognizes who the person is. A few visual clues (their gait, the colour of the coat they were wearing) have been compared with my internal models, and a complete picture of my friend emerges. I *know* who it will be standing outside the door.

Sometimes the frameworks don't work so well. I see a man in the distance walking towards me. The way he walks is somehow familiar and I think it is my old friend whom I haven't seen for ages, and I smile and wave at him. As he moves closer, however, and more visual information becomes available, I suddenly realize (with some embarrassment) that it isn't my old friend at all. Yet just a second ago the figure looked so undeniably like him. It is interesting to pay attention to these kinds of situations. In that moment we can reveal something of the process of perception at work, uncover something of the mind's fabrication. If we watch closely we can sometimes catch the moment when what the mind has constructed falls apart. It is as though a jigsaw puzzle that had successfully been completed, forming a clear picture, disintegrates, and then is reassembled into a new image of a person walking in our direction (giving us a quizzical look, wondering why we were waving at them). The fabric of our world unravels and, just as quickly, is sewn back together again.

In that encounter with my childhood home, my mental framework was outdated. This threw me into confusion for a few moments and strangely confounded my ability to see what was actually there. Those little incidents are fascinating because they reveal the extent to which our world is 'mind made', built by the mind using the raw material (sense data) of the present, but assembling and arranging it according to the blueprint (memories and mental models) of the past. Whilst perceptions of ordinary things like houses will probably be relatively trivial and ethically neutral, there are situations in which the interpretive frameworks that we unconsciously harbour in our minds can have more serious ethical implications.

'Craving stories' and 'aversion stories'

Recently someone I know behaved rudely and inconsiderately towards some friends of mine. As I witnessed this behaviour I became angry, even outraged, and immediately, within a lightning flash of time, a whole interpretation of what they had done exploded in my mind. I knew, or I thought I knew, why this person had acted unskilfully, what their problem was, what their underlying motive had been, and what ought to be done about it. Very quickly I formed a theory about that person and their behaviour. A detailed and complex explanation of their actions had been produced in no time at all. It was devastatingly quick, clear, and cutting. It was also righteous and angry.

Pretty fast, I caught myself and realized what I was doing. I saw that my mind had instantly conjured up a story. This story neatly explained what I didn't like about the person's actions, and justified my feelings about them. But the story was just a story; it was an interpretation that I had imposed onto the objective reality, the actual facts of what had happened. In the heat of the moment, however, it was hard to distinguish between that more objective situation and the interpretation that burnt so fiercely in my mind.

I wondered how I had constructed such an elaborate theory, on the spot, in an instant, without any need for thought or reflection, without any conscious effort. A perfectly formed story had sprung immediately to mind. An explanation just appeared, seemingly out of nowhere. That explanation then became my reality. Where did it come from?

The story was another of my mind's interpretive frameworks, built from layers of past experiences, perceptions, feelings, and emotions. There were probably previous experiences of that person, and stories about them, that my mind had stored away, and which it quickly drew upon. There were, most likely, other stories about similar situations I had encountered, stock explanations and theories about people's motives, that were quickly gathered together and stitched up into an instant explanation, a means to decide how to act in the heat of the moment.

We could view this from a biological, evolutionary perspective: I am confronted with a threatening situation and my life depends on very quickly sizing it up and choosing a course of action. There is no time for reflection. If I reflect, it will be too late. Or an opportunity suddenly presents itself, and again a quick response is required, before my rivals take advantage and the opportunity is gone. Most of us, most of the time, however, are not in situations of immediate danger or opportunity. Yet our minds still react with the same urgency, and we still tend to believe the stories they concoct for us, and then respond, acting or speaking on the basis of our instantaneous theories. This is to act or speak unreflectively, to be determined by our *past*, to have our previous conditioning and experience automatically projected into the present. We repeat the past; we play out the past in the present.

We *do* need to interpret, to take a view on what is happening to us. It is impossible *not* to have a view, interpretation, or story. To say 'I don't know' is just another view. However, we can form views, understandings, and theories that are more clear, perceptive, true, and helpful. Or we can hold views that are more confused, unreflective, slanted and distorted, and unhelpful. Perhaps, usually, what we do with our minds lies somewhere on the spectrum between these two. So what is the difference between these two types of thinking, these two modes of interpretation?

The most crucial and decisive difference is the type of emotion that fuels the explanation – the underlying, perhaps unconscious, volitional force that drives our narrative, pushing the storyline

66

in one direction or another. Some stories are fuelled, either subtly or more strongly, by craving, attachment, self-pity, fear, hatred, irritation, frustration, or other negative emotions. Such emotions *always* produce a distorted perception, a biased and inaccurate story or interpretation. 'Craving stories' exaggerate the pleasant features of a person, object, or situation that we like and desire. 'Aversion stories' exaggerate the features we dislike, find unpleasant, and want to push away.

Perhaps a colleague of mine turns up late to work a few times. This lateness causes me inconvenience, but, despite this, other colleagues don't seem too bothered. I start ruminating on the situation and become resentful. 'He is *always* late', I tell myself over and over again. The next morning at work, 15 minutes before he is due to arrive, a feeling of tense, irritated anticipation arises in my stomach. 'I bet he will be late again!' I am wired to notice lateness. If he does arrive late, this arrival is added to the catalogue of evidence against him, etched clearly in my mind, not to be forgotten. Yet if he turns up on time, I may not even notice, or I even feel a touch disappointed; somehow I manage to discount his punctuality, and so it slips from my mind.

This is a pretty trivial example; but it is an illustration of what we are doing so often: creating stories about the past that determine our experience of the present. As a consequence, we repeat and embellish the story and so create more of the same experiences in the future. 'Aversion stories' are probably easier to spot than 'craving stories' because what they exaggerate is more unpleasant, even painful. They can be more obviously perverse and counterproductive. Despite this, our world is rife with aversion stories that, individually or collectively, are maintained year after year, causing immense suffering. They can become intensely bitter, become like prisons that people are locked into, stories that are no longer stories but absolute and fixed certainties, central to people's identity and reality.

'Craving stories', by contrast, may seem more pleasant and harmless. But they can still be limiting and distracting, or even distorting and harmful. How much time do we waste fantasizing about things we don't really need, or daydreaming about the future, imagining scenarios that always put us in a good light, that are dreamy and unreal, rather than helpful and reflective?

Not long ago I heard of a man who began an affair with the wife of a close friend. Eventually, and inevitably, the affair was discovered, causing pain and division amongst the family and friends of those immediately involved. Some friends of the man asked him why he had done it: it was obvious his behaviour was going to cause trouble. What had possessed him to do such a thing? His reply was to say, sorrowfully, 'I couldn't get her out of my mind.' The affair started with a thought, and then the thought became a story, and then the story became reality. Probably the initial thought seemed innocuous, just an idle fantasy that he allowed to play on in his mind. Desire fed itself into a story; the story then fed the desire and made it stronger. Gradually it became the overriding story of his life, heavily loaded with desire and emotion. When circumstances eventually provided him with an opportunity to act out the story, he couldn't stop himself. It was too late. The story was now so strong that it was destined to come true; the story he had been telling himself for weeks and months created the future.

Again, there is nothing inherently wrong about imagining the future. Obviously it can be good and healthy to have goals and aspirations, and even dreams and big visions about where you want your life to go. It is more a question of the emotions that are driving the imagining and the degree of awareness involved. The future is a story about where we think we're heading, and it can be either a more helpful or a more harmful story. We can't tell how it will actually turn out. The future is unknown; for us right now, it only exists as ideas, hopes, and predictions inside our head. We don't know what will happen tomorrow, let alone next year. This uncertainty can be hard to bear. Perhaps, as a result, our stories about the future often tend to be 'anxiety stories', driven by our dislike of not knowing and craving for a particular outcome. Sometimes, maybe especially if we are of an anxious or pessimistic temperament, our imagination can go into hyperactive mode, leading us to think the worst. If we sign the contract on this flat, we're bound to see a better and cheaper flat the next day. If we go on a long journey, the car will definitely break down. These stories cause us pointless anxiety and suffering, as described by Vessantara in his book *Tales of Freedom*:

> If we look at the number of times throughout our lives we have put ourselves through the pain of imagining terrible things that never actually happened [...] the total represents a huge mass of completely unnecessary suffering [...]. And this comes about because we cannot just think, 'Well, I don't know what is going to happen.' Therefore it is important to stay alert in situations where there is an information vacuum, and allow yourself not to know. Or, if that is really asking too much, at least you can practise filling the space with something positive.[48]

Being defined by our stories, or being aware of them

A friend who suffers from insomnia told me that sometimes, if he wakes up in the morning after an unusually good night's sleep, there can be a sense of relief, but also, oddly, a feeling of annoyance. What has happened doesn't fit with his view of himself as someone who doesn't sleep well. We can become identified with, and attached to, our stories.

Not long ago I was on a coach journey, and a woman in the seat immediately behind me was having a long, loud, and angry conversation on her mobile phone. I found her voice unpleasant and gradually I tipped into aversion. Then, without me quite knowing it, I also slipped into a story, like a hand fitting neatly into a glove. I told myself I wasn't going to enjoy the journey, I didn't like coaches, and it would have been better to travel by train. My experience seemed to confirm the story. The window above me rattled irritatingly. A young man opposite was listening to music on his headphones and the noise was spilling out of them. I looked at my watch and was convinced the coach was running late.

Then, with a little shock, I realized that I was actively looking for these negative experiences. I was *choosing* to pay attention to them. And I was doing this because it fitted my story. I was, automatically and subconsciously, looking for evidence to justify and substantiate my idea of how unpleasant the journey was going to be. I was actively playing out and perpetuating that story. We can become attached to even the small, mean, and limiting stories. I saw how perverse it was to focus on unpleasant experiences and decided to give attention to the more enjoyable aspects of the journey, such as the beautiful autumn colours outside the window, or the way the coach sped smoothly along. Soon the rattle of the window was not at all disruptive, the woman's phone conversation came to a close, and, eventually, the coach arrived right on time.

These examples, and my earlier story about the late colleague, show how we can become identified with our stories. We almost want the evidence to confirm the story, even though that will be unpleasant or inconvenient for us. The pleasure of the story, the little thrill of being in the right, outweighs the pain or inconvenience. We can even end up wanting something unpleasant to happen, in order to prove our story is right. Even though that story is painful and limiting, we feel safe and secure inside it. At least we know, or think we know, that we are in the right. Our stories, our prophecies about our life, become self-fulfilling. And then, because we are attached to our stories, we spend more time polishing and embellishing them, giving them renewed life and lustre.

We can become defined by our stories. Our interpretative frameworks condition what we notice in the world and how we respond, and then our experience tends to confirm that framework. And so round we go again. We become like actors stuck in a role, repeating the same lines, the same scenes, the same drama, night after night. Just as I couldn't see my old house because it didn't fit with what I was anticipating, our perceptions of other people and social situations are conditioned by our expectations and our explanatory frameworks. We have a bias, but it is invisible to us; we don't know what we don't see.

We cannot *not* have a story. I might say to myself: 'The past is gone and unreal so I will live completely in the present.' But that is just another story, another interpretation. As soon as we wake up in the morning, our minds start turning over the day ahead; we start accessing our stories. The first person you meet as you leave home for the day: do you say a cheery good morning, or are you more wary? Your response will be conditioned by memory and by your interpretive framework. It *has* to be; otherwise each and every experience will be new and unknown, and our day will soon become baffling and overwhelming.

However, we can be more aware and reflective around our stories, and especially the underlying emotions that are authoring them. We can stand back and view them from a critical distance. We can either choose stories that incarcerate us, defining ourselves and others more rigidly and tightly, or we can maintain a more free and flexible interpretation. Our frameworks can be small and closed in, giving us only a constricted angle on the world. Or they can be larger and wider, opening up a bigger perspective. Negative emotions create narrow, brittle frameworks; positive emotions give us a broader and more expansive view, one that is much more open and liberating.

Indeed, an essential part of living a happier and more human life is to be aware of our stories, the interpretative frameworks that might otherwise cause us to act out the same old scenes from the same old script. Sometimes we notice our thinking is fast, circular, repetitive, driven, even a touch obsessive and addictive. There is a story, a plot line, and we just can't get it out of our heads. If we start questioning the story or trying to think differently, we can feel the emotional investment in it; our mind swerves back 'on message' as soon as our awareness wavers. The narrative seems to have its own momentum.

Awareness is the key. First of all, if we can keep coming back to our bodily and sensory experience, then we create a little distance from our mind's plotting and scheming; it is being fed a little less energy and its momentum begins to slow. This can then help us become aware of the thinking itself, to feel its energy, notice the emotional tone of the voice telling us the story, and start paying attention to the content. Is it true? Is it exaggerated or biased? Or is there something we are minimizing or skating over? Is it helpful? What have we got invested in this story?

When we are in an emotionally positive state, our thinking can be more easily and naturally aware and reflective. We still make use of the past, but we are more intelligent and questioning. Rather than becoming stuck in that past, we consider how we can respond now, in the present, so as to create a different future. We are more real, more objective, more in touch with the full range of experience, not selecting and denying, exaggerating or minimizing. If we don't want our life to be at the mercy of the same old stories, then we need to be able to tell the difference between these two types of thinking.

Stories can be small and unremarkable, private and personal. Or they can be big collective stories that shape a whole culture and change the course of history. Religions are such stories, sometimes for better, sometimes for worse. Nazism was a story, so were apartheid and communism, so is caste in India. There are social and economic conditions that mean people feel afraid and insecure. Someone articulates a story that explains that fear and gives them someone to blame, or that gives them hope, a way to take responsibility and move forwards. Such powerful stories grip people's imagination. They become the myths that we believe in, and live by, and then they become real.

You may think that some of the examples in this chapter are relatively inconsequential. In a way, they are. Yet they are the stories that tick through our mind second by second, minute by minute, hour by hour. Then the hours become days, the days weeks, and the weeks turn into years. For each of us, those small, ordinary tales that we tell every day become, repeated over years, the overarching narrative of our life. We become our stories.

I am at the time of life we customarily call middle age, during which we can start to feel the passing of time more keenly. I ponder the past, dimly aware of feelings that I can't quite put a name to. Or I feel wistful about once-cherished plans that I know will never come to fruition. The years have passed by so quickly. Life turned out to be so much more bewildering and complex than I imagined when I was young. And so it is tempting to become nostalgic, to dwell sentimentally on the past. Humanly and understandably enough, we can tend to want to remember only the good times, the pleasure and success, not the suffering and failure. Psychologists have studied the bias and selectivity in how we remember: some people seem to cling to the unpleasant and painful, but apparently most people tend to edit out the pain of the past. We create an airbrushed version of our lives. It is like leafing through an old family photo album with rows and rows of faces smiling to camera. It captures something of the past, but there is so much missing. The smiles are only part of the story;

there were also the arguments, the awkwardness, the mutual incomprehension, and, mostly, the humdrum days that have faded from memory. We don't want to be reminded of that, or of the compromise and disappointment. We are our past; it becomes a part of our identity, of how we like to think of ourselves and define who we are.

The interconnectedness of past, present, and future

We interpret the present according to the past. We also reinterpret the past according to the present. And both processes then condition the future. Past, present, and future are not as fixed and separate as we might think: they are always colouring each other. However, we are not totally trapped in a time loop, not absolutely caught up in closed circles of determinism. We have the light of awareness; we can see and step back from our inner narrative. Awareness isn't absolute either, at least not to begin with. Our conditioning will influence what it is that we are able to see, or not see. But we can choose to look, train ourselves to look, we can gradually increase our awareness and break free of the past, which can create a new future.

In other words, memory has an ethical dimension. What we remember about an interaction or incident is a story that we told ourselves. That story would have been loaded, one way or the other, by emotions and volitions: craving or aversion, or acceptance and kindness. The story has ethical implications for the future. Memory is evaluation. We remember according to what we value, or how we have evaluated our experience; those memories then help us place value on what happens next. We can also re-evaluate; we can re-examine stories we have been telling all our life.

Considering memory in this way, looking at how humans tell stories (both privately in their own heads and collectively), and at how past, present, and future all mutually recondition each other, raises interesting questions about identity. Who am I? Where in time does my identity reside? Is it just in the present? That present is never the same for more than a moment, which would mean my identity is not at all stable or enduring. In that case, am I also my past? Does my identity reside in who I have been? If so, then how much of the past do I include: today, the last week, the previous year, my whole lifetime? Am I just some, or all, of that past? What about the parts that I can't remember? Are they included? Every second that passes means I have more past, so again this doesn't make for a very stable or enduring identity. At every moment future is becoming past, so do I include my future in my sense of identity? But that future doesn't yet exist!

Examining self-identity from a temporal perspective raises some strange questions. Just who are we? One of the most striking, distinctive, and perhaps counterintuitive teachings of the Buddha was that of *anātman* – usually translated as 'no self' or 'no fixed self'. It was this ever changing nature of self-identity that he was getting at. Who I am is never fixed, final, or completely definable.[49] I may tell a story about the past; but, for me now, that past no longer exists, and neither does the 'me' that features in the story. I may have a story about the future; but, for me now, that doesn't exist either, nor does the 'me' around which the story revolves.

Imagine a river flowing swiftly along until it comes to a sudden edge where the water plunges down to the rocks below. That sheer edge of the waterfall is what we call the present. We naturally identify with that edge; that, we say, is *me*, that is where *I* am right now. From this point of view, what is behind is the past, the surging weight of habit and circumstance flooding in upon us. What is in front of us is the future, a leap into the unknown. The edge, that crisp white cusp of water, seems so clearly delineated, so real. But it is made from millions of swirling water particles, cascading onwards, past tumbling into future, over the knife-edge of the present. Nothing about that edge remains the same for more than a moment. Actually, it is the very speed of the flow that gives it such a solid and substantial appearance. There is, however, nothing there now that was there a moment ago, or that will still be there in another moment. So where am I? Who am I? The edge? Or the river? Or something else again?

When we tell a story about the past or future, we tend to project ourselves *as we are now* into that past or future. It may be helpful to have a plan (which is a kind of story) for my future. But I know that such a plan is just a story; the future won't be absolutely as I predict, and I won't be who I predict either. In a certain sense, it won't be my future. It will be that of some other unknowable being who doesn't yet exist! If I can stay open and flexible in this way, I can keep the future more open and flexible. I can have a dream about the future, without getting fixated on it. I can also remember my past, but without being rigidly defined by my story. I can just let the past be the past, and let the future be the future.

Each of us could be described as a bundle of stories about the past, being articulated in the present, and thereby leading us towards a particular future. However, we are not *just* those stories; there is also awareness, there is something outside the story, not defined by the story. That awareness makes freedom possible. The following chapter considers how this works in practice. It includes an inspiring example of someone who has re-evaluated her history, transformed her relationship with the story of her past. We can free the past and free the future.

5 o'clock

Healing time

I have a friend who, as a child, was abused, physically and verbally, by her two parents who suffered from alcoholism. Through her childhood years, Bec endured the rage of her unpredictable mother and father. The home environment was unimaginably unstable and chaotic, and this undermined any sense of my friend being able to trust others, or any self-worth or confidence she had. The child-protection authorities never intervened. Bec told me that as a teenager she wrote a diary to herself and each day's entry ended with these words: 'Please God, get me out of here.'

One day, aged twenty-three, she had been attending a social event at her place of work. As she left her workplace, she saw her drunken parents clambering into their car. It was their wedding anniversary and they had been out to celebrate. Despite the warnings of her friends, Bec joined her parents, climbed into the back of the car, and they drove off home together. Not long afterwards, her father stopped the car. He and her mother were furious that their daughter had not been present to celebrate their wedding anniversary. In an alcoholic rage, her father dragged Bec from the car and beat her up, while her mother threw things at her and hurled abuse from the sidelines. They drove off, leaving her, bloodied and bruised, lying in the gutter, severely traumatized.

A passing taxi driver saw my friend there and pulled over. He told her he was going to call the police. 'Please don't do that,' she pleaded, 'they're my parents.' Deeply shocked at this, the taxi driver told Bec he would take her anywhere she needed to go. At her request, he dropped her off at her friend's house where she could recover. To this day she feels grateful to that taxi driver. She moved away and vowed she would never forgive her parents. They had done her so much damage. They were utterly untrustworthy. She never wanted anything to do with them again.

Six weeks later Bec walked into the London Buddhist Centre and began to learn to meditate. She was angry, armoured, not even contemplating the possibility of forgiveness. But, over time, chinks were beginning to open up in that armour. One day someone asked her when she was going to forgive her parents. 'When they are sorry' was Bec's defiant response. 'What if they are never sorry?' came the rejoinder. This made her think. What if they were never sorry? Was she going to carry on feeling righteously angry for the rest of her days?

Buddhist practice and being part of the sangha (spiritual community) kept prising open those chinks in Bec's defensive shell. She went to see Sangharakshita, her Buddhist teacher, and asked him if she needed to forgive her parents. He leant forwards and looked at her kindly, but also very directly. 'Yes, you *must* forgive them', he said emphatically. He also told her that it didn't matter if they were alive or dead, she just needed to attempt that work of forgiveness.

This task proved to be a twenty-year undertaking. Meditating in front of her shrine, Bec asked the Buddhas to give her the strength to forgive and understand. She worked in her meditation to develop loving-kindness (*mettā*). This entailed acknowledging painful feelings and giving herself loving-kindness, and also trying to encourage a kind, helpful, understanding attitude towards her parents. But it was reflecting on the Buddhist teaching of the three *lakṣaṇas*[50] that she found most transformative. This pivotal teaching tells us that all worldly things are impermanent, therefore none of them can give us lasting satisfaction, nor can any of them have an enduring, fixed essence or self. My friend Bec reflected on the pain that her past had caused her, and she realized that her parents, too, must be suffering pain. She reflected again and again on impermanence, reminding herself that she was not the same person as all those years ago, and nor were her parents the same people. Moreover, the undeniable truth of impermanence meant that they would all one day die, and none of them knew who would die first, or when. Bec realized she did not want to die without having forgiven her parents, and this deepened her motivation.

Eventually, during a retreat, reflecting on the third *lakṣaṇa* of *anātman*, or 'no fixed self', she experienced an even more decisive breakthrough, a moment of utter clarity. She saw clearly that the twenty-three-year-old who had climbed into the back of her parents' car on that fateful day no longer existed. Bec wasn't denying her past or her pain, but she now knew that the young woman was no longer; if she looked within, she could not find her anymore. She was gone. If she couldn't find her, then why was there all that anger and pain? Bec realized she had spent years repeating to herself, over and over again, the story of that young woman. She had done it in order to fuel the anger. What would it be like to stop doing that? How would it be if she dropped the story?

For my friend, it has been important to bear witness, to speak the emotional truth of her past trauma. But that bearing witness has also been somewhat complex. She now understood that it was chiefly the anger and resentment that had prevented her from forgiving for twenty years. However, there was also a fear that forgiving would somehow mean failing to bear witness to the young girl she had once been, somehow denying her story. She began to see that there was a danger of confusing bearing witness with something much less helpful – attachment to her story, clinging tightly to her version of what had happened. She had to let go of that attachment.

At last my friend wrote to her mother. She said that she didn't want one of them to die without there having been forgiveness. She explained that she didn't want to talk about anything in the past, but just to forgive her. Eventually she met her mother, and has since written, in a similar vein, to her father too. She remains in regular contact with both of them. As far as she was concerned, there was no need for any explanation or apology. She knew in her heart that she no longer felt like a victim. In fact, she could see that her parents were the real victims, that their lives had been the more wasted and tragic.

Of course the events of her childhood still affect her; there are deeply engrained, almost instinctual, emotional responses she learnt, conditioning that she will be working to transform for the rest of her life. But Bec has also made the most extraordinary and inspiring changes. She has many good friendships and relationships in her life, a supportive marriage, a successful career in criminal justice. She has become an ordained member of a Buddhist sangha. To some extent she still is a *product* of her past. But she is not a *victim* of it.

Forgiving, but not forgetting

The past exists only in our memories. What we remember, the subtleties of how we remember, and how we relate to those memories are partly a matter of choice. We can change how we remember. We can, in effect, travel back in time and change the past. Or, at least, we can go back and cut through the chains so that the past has much less hold over us.

Some emotions are like chains, shackling us to a version of history. Guilt, self-pity, blame: these negative emotions keep us at the mercy of our past. They are essentially self-referential; they are concerned with what was done to *me*, how unfair others were to *me*. Such emotions create, and then circle round, a small, tight knot of self. They produce stories and interpretations that are essentially self-perpetuating, confining, and claustrophobic. When we tell ourselves we have been a victim in the past, we will become a victim *of* the past, and that past becomes the jailer of our future. Other emotions, such as forgiveness and apology, are able to smash down the door, cut through the chains, and set us free. They don't gloss over the past or ignore the pain – but they refuse to be tied to it, or defined by it.

According to the Buddhist text known as the *Dhammapada*, the unwise 'brood over the past like aged herons in a pond without fish'.[51] When some people tell us their story, we can feel it is highly subjective; it is a slanted view, leaning over with heavy emotion, a story told by someone still intensely weighed upon by their past. The emotions with which their story is loaded may be humanly understandable, but if the teller is full of self-pity, this is draining and exhausting for all. Other people's stories, although very open and personal, are more 'objective'. They are told with more balance, more sense of resolution with respect to the past. We sense someone who seems to be more in control of their lives, more responsible for their future. These are the stories that have more insight and perspective, and, rather than draining energy and shutting us down, these stories inspire, energize, and open our hearts.

If we want a healthy relationship to our history, if we want to be more free in respect of our past, then we will need forgiveness. Sometimes we need to forgive ourselves. Sometimes we need to forgive others. The Buddhist word that comes closest in meaning to our word 'forgiveness' is *kṣānti*,[52] which means something like 'unaffected by' or 'able to withstand'. It is usually translated as 'patience', 'forbearance', 'tolerance', and also as 'forgiveness'. Forgiveness is to forbear, even when a wrong has been done to us, even though it may be painful. It is not to downplay that wrong, or to deny the feeling of pain. But we don't let those feelings take us into a state of ill will or hatred, of wanting to inflict pain back, of wanting revenge. The English word 'forgiveness' has a similar etymology: the prefix 'for' means 'abstention' or 'renunciation'. To 'for-give' is to 'abstain from giving', to not need or wish to return in kind what has been 'given' or done to us. It is to drop any desire to 'get even', or to take revenge.

How can we practise forgiveness?[53] A well-known saying states that the cynic neither forgives nor forgets, the naïve forgive and forget, whilst the wise forgive but do not forget.[54]

For some people, what has happened to them can be so painful that they try to shut down their heart; they tell themselves that the best way to avoid future hurt is to withhold their trust of others. This stance can then, over time, harden into underlying negativity, resentment, and cynicism. For other people, however, there might be a tendency towards prematurely laying aside the issue; they try to tell themselves: 'It doesn't matter, I'm not bothered, I'm not going to be affected by this.' They are trying to forget as a way of pushing the pain away and not having to feel it. Forgiveness crucially involves having loving-kindness towards our self and our pain, as well as towards others. The first step to healing and forgiveness is to accept our hurt, acknowledge the pain. This, of course, may take time and is not always easy.

Then, perhaps, we can begin to 'forgive but not forget'. We still remember what happened, but we are able to let it be, without fighting the felt truth of our experience and angrily wanting the other person and the situation to have been different. We might never be able to understand others' past motivations. However, through practising a meditation such as the *mettā bhāvanā*,[55] we may start to see the common humanity that others share with us – that each is a person born into certain conditioning, someone who can take wrong turnings as well as right ones, someone with hopes and fears, another human being struggling through life to be happy. Maybe we start to understand more sympathetically the circumstances of others' lives, how the dice might have been loaded in a way that made certain actions of theirs more likely.

Often, before we can forgive others, we need to forgive ourselves. We can sometimes blame ourselves for what took place, or we tell ourselves it happened because we're bad and unworthy and deserved it. Maybe our actions did play a part in what happened; perhaps we recognize that we were gullible or foolish. But that doesn't mean it was 'deserved' and, anyway, we don't need to be forever defined by our past actions. We all make mistakes and we need to forgive ourselves, show ourselves understanding and kindness.[56]

So forgiveness is not forgetting. It is more a re-remembering, a transformation of how we tell the story of what happened, and of how rigidly we define a person by what they once did, or rigidly define ourselves by what was done to us and the pain we suffered. To forgive is to remember within a bigger space of awareness and kindness, within a more expansive perspective. It is certainly not being a 'doormat'. Although we are trying to forgive and not give way to hatred, there may also be situations that we need to confront, injustices we decide to take a stand against. We can forgive someone as well as pointing out to them the harm they have done and urging them to stop. Forgiveness makes us better able to challenge injustice, rather than giving in to despair, anger, and frustration. Hatred, self-pity, resentment: these negative emotions block and waste so much emotional energy. Forgiveness sets our heart free; it releases energy and makes it available for more positive causes.

There are extraordinary cases of people forgiving even in the most extreme circumstances. For example, there is the inspiring story of Bud Welch, whose daughter was killed in a terrorist bomb attack in the USA in the 1990s.[57] At first he sank into self-destructive anger and hatred, but eventually he was able to forgive the bomber, and even helped campaign (unsuccessfully) for him not to receive the death penalty. He also befriended the father of the young man who committed the atrocity. Bud Welch said that this man had lost more than he had. Welch himself had lost his daughter, but he could still talk openly about her, and rejoice in her life. This man had lost his son, as well as any ease in ever referring to him. Bud Welch also explained that initially many people demanded that the young man receive the death penalty for his crime. However, as time went on, more and more people realized his execution would benefit no one. After the execution, even more people realized his death hadn't helped them or anyone else. It didn't help them heal. Another death achieved nothing at all.

Wholehearted forgiveness can be very challenging and difficult. It requires a willingness to bear pain; to forbear for the sake of a greater good. Forgiveness may not always take away that pain, at least not immediately. But it stops us being trapped and defined by it, and this will tend to lessen and soften it over time.

Without forgiveness, the thread of our life may remain severed at certain junctures. The time that is our life may feel chopped and broken. Forgiveness ties the threads of our life together again into one flowing whole. That thread may not be smooth and perfect at the joins, but perhaps more gnarled and knotted. Those knots, however, serve as reminders of work well done, lessons hard won, of the time spent healing those old wounds and bonding the arc of our life back into a continuous whole.

Forgiveness brings light into the darkness; it is an act of supreme courage and generosity. It changes the story of our past, from one of self-pity to one of compassion for self and other. Past becomes future through the prism of the present. We can't change certain basic facts about the past. We can change, in the present, the story we tell about them. And, in doing this, we can free the future.

6 o'clock

River time

Imagine that our planet earth is magically transferred to another solar system. In its new location it revolves on its axis quicker, so that a day on new earth is shorter than a day used to be on old earth. Similarly, the planet circles the sun on a quicker orbit, so that the seasons change faster, and a year is shorter than on old earth.

By some bizarre coincidence, it takes 365 of the new, shorter days for new earth to rotate round the sun, just as it took 365 of the old, longer days for old earth to revolve round its sun. So a year still comprises 365 days, but they are shorter days and shorter years than in the previous solar system.

At first, everything about life on new earth seems pretty much the same. The planet and its inhabitants have come through this stellar relocation remarkably well, seemingly unaffected. There is only one other significant change: when the relocation occurred, every single timekeeping device in the world recalibrated itself such that they all matched the new shorter days and years. An hour on a clock is still one twenty-fourth of the time it takes for the earth to rotate on its axis.

What would our experience of time be like on new earth? Even though our clocks have recalibrated and still show a day as 24 hours, and even though a year is still 365 days, surely we would notice that the days and years were shorter? Baking a potato in the oven used to take 90 minutes. But if we took a potato out of the oven after 1.5 hours on new earth, it would still be hard in the middle. A journey to see a friend in a faraway city used to be a day's travelling on old earth. Now, when nightfall comes, we find we still have miles to go. We would notice numerous differences. Not only would recipe books need serious editing, there would be a myriad of discrepancies between the old time and the new. By constrast, whilst on old earth a good life expectancy was 80 years, here on new earth we will still feel relatively youthful and spritely at 80 and hope to live till at least 120. However, we will have to wait until we are 95 before we can claim our pension.

Would the shorter days and years make us feel we had less time or more? Our clocks have recalibrated themselves to the shorter hours and days, and this means the hands of a clock travel faster round the face of that clock than they would have done on old earth. Would we feel that time was going faster? Or would we know that it made no difference: we have the same time, it is just that the new motion of planet earth and the change in our timekeeping devices divides the time up differently? Would we rush to get things done within a shorter day, or would we go slower? If we had been relocated to a planet with *longer* days and years than on old earth, would it have made those days feel more spacious? Or would the fact that now, on average, a person lives for only fifty years make life seem more quick and fleeting?

This thought experiment is an attempt to tease out the real nature of time. The opening chapter of this book examined our subjective experience of time: that bus journey to visit my friend may seem long and tedious if I am bored, or it may seem to pass more quickly if I am enjoying myself, perhaps zipping along listening to music that I love. However, isn't it true that, travelling at a given speed, the journey takes a fixed amount of time, regardless of our subjective feelings about it? Don't we believe that there is an objective time that it takes to complete the journey?

Chapter 2 considered the measurement of clock time. To measure time, we have to compare and calibrate. Our time-measuring customs date back to pre-mechanical cultures and were originally derived from natural cycles: sunrise and sundown, the changing seasons, the phases of the moon. Time measurement then became more mechanical and linear, more removed from the natural, observable rhythms that were part of human life and experience. Clocks measured time according to the swing of a pendulum or, later still, the vibrations of a sliver of quartz subjected to a tiny electrical current. By comparing events in our life with the position of the sun, or the hands of a clock rotating, or the numbers on a digital display changing, we say that the event happened at a certain time, or took so much time. However, this calibrating isn't time itself; it is just a convention for measuring and comparing events and happenings. Clocks 'keep' time, but what is being kept and where? Clocks 'tell' the time, but what are they *really* telling us?

On new earth the days and years are shorter, and all the mechanical timekeeping devices were recalibrated accordingly. This means the journey to visit my friend in the distant city now takes more hours. Despite this, however, I know that the journey doesn't really take more *time*. 'Mechanical clock time' obviously isn't real time; it is simply a way of calibrating and measuring.

'Organic clock time' – the cycles of night and day, winter and summer – may be less abstract and closer to our sensory experience than mechanical clock time. Yet this thought experiment shows that organic time isn't real time either. On new earth days and seasons come and go quicker. The journey that on old earth took a day now takes a day and a half. But, again, I know that the time spent travelling isn't actually, objectively, any longer.

It is quite likely that we still feel and believe that there is an *objective* time that it takes to bake a potato, complete a journey of 500 miles, or live a human lifespan. Time isn't *just* a purely subjective experience, and clock time (mechanical or organic) isn't time itself either, just a convention for measuring and calibrating something. So what is being measured and calibrated? What is time?

Time is change, or transiency. And transiency is what we call time, what we *feel* as time passing. Organic time measures changes that we perceive (raw potato becoming cooked potato, for example) by comparing and referring to changes in natural cycles. Clock time also measures changes by comparing with mechanical or electronic changes inside the clock. To measure and compare change, we need a reference point. Humans make use of what is naturally around them (such as the location of the sun in the sky), or something they have constructed themselves (the position of a shadow cast by the sun on a dial, the motion of a pendulum, or the vibrations of a piece of quartz), in order to be able to measure change and duration.

There is our subjective, psychologically conditioned experience of time. In addition, there are conventionally agreed upon, culturally constructed, reference points for measuring time. Neither of these, however, is time itself. Time is transiency. And if time is transiency, time is also transformation, in the simplest and most profound sense.

How we talk about time and change

Let us look more closely at what is being said here. We experience change – events happening and processes unfolding – and we use the *idea* of time in order to be able to make sense of our experience and talk about it. Say we experience events X ...Y... ... ... Z. We can talk about the proximity of these events; we say that there was a 'short' time between events X and Y. They happened 'close together'. And we say that there was a 'long' time between Y and Z. They were 'further apart'. We can also say that event Y happened 'before' Z but 'after' X; we can place events in an order.

Notice that these ways of talking about the three events all employ *spatial* imagery: long or short, close or far apart, before or after. It seems that we always resort to spatial comparisons in order to conceive of time. Actually there are two main metaphors we employ.[58] Either we think of ourselves as moving through time, along a line of time. Or else we envisage time passing or flowing past us. In the first metaphor we move through, or along, our life, as though we are on a raft drifting downriver, and we pass by people, houses, and places – the events of our life – on the riverbank. In the second metaphor, we are on the riverbank watching the river of our life – and all the contents of that life – flowing by.

When we say something such as 'it seems ages since we last went on holiday', or 'it won't be long before it's time to leave for the airport', we are using the first metaphor. When we say things like 'the week in France sped by really quickly', or 'we waited a long time before the bus turned up', we are using the second. These are really two versions of the same spatial metaphor. Either we are moving along a line observing ourselves approaching nearer, then passing, and then moving away from, events in time. Or events in time are moving along a line whilst we watch them coming closer and then receding into the distance. Either we observe as we pass by events, or we watch from one side as events pass us by.

The way we talk about time, or about change, seems (in the English language at least) to involve the use of spatial metaphor. Intrinsic to this way of conceiving change are two components. One is 'me' observing that change, watching things pass by whilst remaining unchanged myself. But of course we are not separate from change – we are part of it. The person who arrived for a week's holiday in France is different from the person who travels home again. This links us back to the Buddha's teaching of *anātman* ('no fixed self'), which we touched on in the last chapter. The other intrinsic part of how we conceive change is that it takes place *in* time, as if there were a medium, invisible in itself, in which life and change are happening. We separate 'me' from 'time'. For now we are going to focus more on this idea of time as a separate medium.

We think we are in time, in a medium of time, like fishes swimming, living, and breathing in water. We are moving through it, or it is flowing past us. We imagine this medium to be real, objective, separate from us, and yet all around us – the container of time in which we exist. But time isn't an external medium. We conventionally say that 'time passes', making time into a 'thing' separate from passing. But could there be a time that does not pass? Here I am paraphrasing from another poem by Jaan Kaplinski:

> The wind does not blow. The wind is the process of blowing
>   itself.
> Can there be a wind that does not blow? Sun that does not
>   shine?
> A river that does not flow? Time that does not flow?
> For time is flux. But no one knows what it is that
> flows. Or can there suddenly be
> time that waits, that remains in one place like the lake
> behind the dam?[59]

Meditators talk about watching 'the breath', but there is really no such thing, only *breathing*, a continuous series of movements of body and air. In the same way, we talk about 'the flow of time', but there is no such thing, only flowing. That metaphor of the flow of time – so commonly used – turns out to be problematic when examined closely. 'Flow' is how fast or slow a liquid is moving. After the rains, a river flows swiftly; during a drought its flow is slow and languid. If you placed a stick on the water's surface and measured how far downriver it floated in one minute, this would be a good way to determine the river's rate of flow. Perhaps in the first case the stick is swept 100 metres in a minute, but in the latter case it drifts for a mere 25; that is how you can compare and say the river flowed four times faster after the rainfall than during the drought.

What, then, does it mean to talk about the flow of time? How fast or slow does time flow? How far does it flow in an hour, how far in a minute? All we can say is that it flows one hour in an hour, or one minute per minute. But this is just tautology. To speak of the passage of time, of its flowing and passing, comes so naturally to us, yet what are we really saying?

Time does not pass; time *is* the process of passing itself. It is not that things change because time passes. Rather, we have the experience of time passing because things change, because we experience change and transformation. We feel the change, the passing; we compare the different ways things change or endure, and we call this time.

Part of what we have been uncovering in this chapter is the limitations of language, which is structured around fixed and separate subjects and objects – like the 'me' witnessing events passing by in 'time'. In reality, there is no aloof, independent vantage point from which I can look out on the world. From the Buddhist point of view, the ignorance and craving that bind us and prevent the true potential of our minds from shining forth go deeper than language; language and thought are not themselves the root of the problem. Yet perhaps they can complicate and reinforce our tendency to think in terms of fixed and separate 'things' instead of ever changing 'processes'. We can tend to forget just how deeply metaphorical our language is.

Free Time!

Understanding time as change and transiency also means that, if we want to investigate our relationship with time, we need to examine our relationship with that change and transiency. The next chapter explores how reflecting on change and examining our emotions and attitudes in respect of the contingent and fleeting nature of life have always been a central concern of Buddhist practice.

7 o'clock

Change time

All this discussion about swapping solar systems, about the metaphorical language of time, and of whether it is true that time really flows can be reduced to two simple ideas. Firstly, there is what we could call 'objective time'. We are part of a world of change, and most of that change is beyond our control. Some changes are welcome to us, other changes we would rather avoid. Yet things will change, certain events will happen, whether we like it or not. This changing-ness and transiency are what, for now, we are calling 'objective time'.

How we respond to that changing-ness helps determine our subjective experience of it. In chapter 1 we looked at how craving and aversion create our inner sense of time. Longing for a change to happen (having aversion to the present state of things and craving some other future state) slows and elongates our experience of time. Longing to avoid a change (clinging to the present and being averse to some alternative future state) speeds up and compresses our sense of time. If, however, we can be more relaxed and less controlling about change, if we are equanimous about both present and future, then our sense of time is likely to be more smooth, open, and flowing. So the second idea to take forward is that we have an inward experience of time that is produced, at least in part, by our attitude to change.

From 'objective time' – events and processes – and depending on our response to those changing circumstances, is created 'subjective time', our inner experience of time. This is the time that we actually live in, the time that is our lived and felt reality. Our attitude to change therefore profoundly affects our time; it radically influences the speed of our life, it determines how temporally spacious or cramped our existence is. It seems important to look at our relationship with change, at how we deal with the contingent, transient nature of life.

Why the Buddha taught impermanence

Our galaxy, very commonly known as the Milky Way, began coming into existence not long after the Big Bang, around 13.8 billion years ago. Eventually it formed into a vast spiral of at least 100 billion stars, and it is still producing new generations of stars from dense clouds of hydrogen gas located in its spiral arms. Assuming there is no collision with another galaxy, it will go on evolving for many billions of years yet. Eventually, however, the hydrogen will run out, no new stars will form, and those that are left will slowly burn up their fuel and cool and then die. The Milky Way's immensely long life will draw to a close.

Planet earth is situated about halfway out from the centre of this galaxy. It is continually bombarded by 'cosmic radiation' from deep space. This radiation crashes into atoms in the earth's upper atmosphere, smashing them into even smaller pieces. The resultant subatomic particles are highly unstable. Even one of the longer-lasting particles such as a muon (which is a bit like a heavy electron) decays within a few millionths of a second of its creation.

An adult mayfly lives for only a couple of days, just long enough to mate and for the females to lay their eggs on the surface of a river or lake, whereas a tortoise can live for 120 years, and there are records of them living for over 175 years in zoos. There is a bristlecone pine in North America that is said to be over 5,000 years old, and the Llangeryw Yew in North Wales is estimated to be 4,000 to 5,000 years in age. If you went back to the time of the Buddha, Confucius, and Socrates, and then as far back in time again, those trees would have been young saplings, just starting out on their long lease of life. In a desert environment, by contrast, plants must adapt to the harsh climate and infrequent rainfall, and some of them, known as 'desert ephemerals', have evolved extremely short lifespans. Their seeds lie dormant in the earth, but then, when the rain falls, they can germinate, grow, flower, pollinate, and set seed, all within a couple of weeks. The plant soon withers away under the drying wind and scorching sun, but its seeds lie in wait for the next brief rainfall, and their chance to sprout into life.

Sometimes, tragically, a human child dies at birth; sometimes that child lives for over a century. A galaxy and a subatomic particle, a mayfly and a tortoise, a bristlecone pine and a desert ephemeral, a stillborn child and a centenarian: a span of life may be long or short, but everything that is born will die. Nothing lasts forever. Everything changes. The rate of change may vary, but the fact of change remains unaltered.

Humans have built whole civilizations and complex technologies to protect themselves against uncertainty and unwelcome change. From the earliest days, they have also created myths and religions to try and understand death and mortality. Buddhist cultures across Asia could likewise be viewed as great contemplations on impermanence. According to the Buddha, really seeing impermanence is a key to understanding both our suffering and our potential liberation from that suffering. Above the entranceway to many Buddhist temples will be displayed a painting or carved image of the wheel of life, a visual representation of the cycles of life and death according to Indo-Tibetan Buddhist cosmology. The wheel is gripped by a gross, fanged, fierce monster. He is Yama, the lord of death. Traditionally, he is also Avalokiteśvara, the bodhisattva of compassion. The figure just appears to us to be Yama because we don't understand death's true nature.

From the unenlightened perspective, impermanence is terrifying: it means loss, devastation, decay, and death. But, from another perspective, impermanence is also freedom. It means change is possible, nothing is fixed or static, nothing ever comes to a final end; all is open and transformable, always full of potential. A short, aphoristic poem by William Blake illustrates these two fundamentally different attitudes to change:

He who binds to himself a joy
Does the winged life destroy;
But he who kisses the joy as it flies
Lives in eternity's sunrise.[60]

Living as we do in a universe of constant change and transiency, holding on to things, trying to grasp them, seeing them as 'mine' in any lasting or absolute sense, is delusory. We can't really, ever, own anything.[61] Nothing finally belongs to me. Craving and attachment are counter to how the universe works; they are out of harmony with the true nature of things. We don't need to hypothesize any outside agency punishing craving or rewarding non-attachment; craving will eventually lead to frustration, disappointment, and suffering through its own logic, or as its own consequence, simply because it is out of synch with how the universe works. Craving will destroy the 'winged life', both that of the desired object and that of our own hearts and minds. To bind ourselves to a joy is to try and freeze time.

Binding to ourselves a joy

A commonplace illustration of how this can happen is the tourist who rushes about with their camera, clicking away, trying to 'capture' the experience, but not actually giving themselves time to savour the experience in the first place. They snap away, perhaps imagining the beautiful picture that they will show to friends back home, but don't pause to gaze up into the vast roof space of the cathedral, or listen to the deep roar of the waterfall, or sit quietly imagining the life of the person depicted in the painting that hangs before them. They may have flown thousands of miles to be in that place, but they never approach close to the 'winged life' that is waiting there for them. To do so, they would need to let go of the desire to capture an experience, and just wander slowly, or sit quietly, so as to really take it in.

It is easy to chuckle at the stereotypical tourist, but how much of our lives is lived in this way? Perhaps we are constantly busy, always, like that tourist, hectic and headed somewhere in the future. In this mode it can feel difficult to make time for other people. Perhaps our elderly father calls for a chat, but whilst he talks we are glancing anxiously at our watch, hoping he will finish soon. We are not fully giving him our care and attention. As a result, when we put the phone down, we feel slightly tangled and disconnected inside. And so, probably, does our elderly parent. The 'winged life' is a shared life of love and intimacy that needs *time*; otherwise people cease to be living, feeling human beings and become mere objects, impediments to completing the numerous tasks we may well have overidentified with.

Or perhaps we are in a relationship where there is insecurity, and then neediness and clinging. Neither person allows the other to be who they are and, again, the winged life of that relationship is diminished. Perhaps we cling onto possessions or people because we think they augment our sense of identity, worth, or status; but we end up feeling trapped, as though our wings have been clipped, and something in us can't quite take flight.

Or again, when enjoying a pleasurable experience, we want the pleasure to continue. So we attempt to repeat the experience; we think we can have the pleasure all over again. In this way we try to 'bind' it to ourselves. We drink a glass of wine, it is pleasant, and so we pour another, subconsciously hoping to repeat the experience. However, because our senses, including our taste buds, are wired for newness and novelty, the second glass is never as enjoyable as the first. Now, slightly more desperate to recapture that earlier pleasure, we pour another glass, this time a larger one. There is a law of diminishing returns at work, and we know how the story ends! We need to practise what a friend of mine calls 'the discipline of delight',[62] knowing that pleasure is 'winged'; it isn't repeatable or graspable. True delight involves an element of constraint and contentment. It involves an implicit awareness of the transient nature of experience, including pleasurable ones. We know that sensory pleasures can't give lasting satisfaction; yet we can, at the same time, relish the sweetness of the day without worrying that it may be gone tomorrow. (In its extreme form, this grasping pattern of behaviour becomes an addiction, which can be devastatingly destructive of that winged life.)

Recently I read an article describing the five most common regrets of people who knew they were dying, as witnessed and recorded by Bronnie Ware, a nurse who worked with many such people during the last twelve weeks of their lives.[63] As death approached, they saw with great clarity what really mattered to them: to live their own life, not the life that others expected or hoped for them; to have spent less time and energy at work; to have had the courage to express feelings and emotions; to have stayed in touch with old friends and prioritized family and friendship. Lastly, they wished they could have lived with less fear of change, not stuck so closely to what seemed safe and comfortable, and realized instead that happiness comes from *how* we live and the choices we make.

To live in the mode of 'binding to ourselves a joy' means to try and hold on to time, which means that time then has a hold over us. We become slaves of time, always trying to escape its dragging and rushing. We need to learn to live in a 'pouring-away world of no attachment',[64] to allow life to fly, not to hold it too tightly, not to be overattached. Notice that this doesn't entail a state of neutral indifference: when we live this way there is *more* passion; we 'kiss the joy as it flies'! We are no longer holding on to time, and so no longer trapped within it.

Sometimes, when we truly, deeply love something and are absorbed by it, we forget all about time, we flow along in harmony with it, even as it changes. We 'live in eternity's sunrise'. In another of his poetic works Blake writes cryptically that: 'Eternity is in love with the productions of time.'[65] If we look at the world with the eyes of a lover, then we meet a world of endless beauty, variety, and fascination. We notice, and are drawn into, the uniqueness of things, their 'minute particulars' (to quote Blake again), including their mutability and change. In fact, 'eternity is in love with the productions of time' precisely *because* of that change and mutability, because each production of time is unique and unrepeatable. It is that unrepeatability, the 'once-only-ness' of life, that gives each moment its preciousness and value. If we can love like that, completely *with* the wave of change, so that we are not separate from it, time can dissolve and deepen into 'eternity'.

'If the doors of perception were cleansed, everything would appear to man as it is, infinite' is yet another of Blake's memorable sayings.[66] If we fully and totally understand and accept impermanence, then we no longer experience 'things' that are separate from each other, and that change in steps and stages into other 'things'. We experience instead an unbroken, unbounded flow, which includes everything, and which we ourselves are not separate from.[67]

Each of us may have had glimpses, or intimations, of that possibility and potential. But in this world with so many practical considerations and responsibilities to attend to, we may not glimpse it very often. Even so, we can still practise 'kissing the joy as it flies'; we can try to live understanding and respecting change and transiency. In this way, even when we need to operate in the world of clock time, we can be less slavish, less oppressed by it.

These lines by Blake might be misunderstood as advocating a headlong, hedonistic rush at life: life is short, so pump the pleasure up to maximum before time runs out. Live like there's no tomorrow. Like the tourist rushing from one destination to another, the hedonist squeezes time as hard as they can, trying to pummel as much juice out of it as possible. They grab a quick kiss while they can, before the joy flies past them. But to live like this is just another 'binding' of pleasure. Such a person is still trapped in time, oppressed and dictated to by the fleetingness of things. In the sense intended by Blake, there is no urgent greed or grasping; there is just a kiss and joy *flying*. Real joy requires *abandonment*: that we abandon that small self that tries to use things (and people) to reinforce an egoistic sense of 'me' and 'mine'. True and deep passion stems from abandonment, letting go, or renunciation of ego-centredness.

8 o'clock

Reflection time

How can we develop a healthy relationship to change? How can we live more aware of, and in harmony with, the ephemeral, impermanent nature of life? In the Buddhist tradition there are many reflections and contemplation practices designed to help us do this. What follows in this chapter is a brief and simple introductory guide to contemplating impermanence, including some different ways we might go about this, and the effects we might observe.[68]

An important factor to bear in mind is that any practice, including contemplation practice, works only within a *context*. This context will include other practices that one is undertaking (such as loving-kindness meditation or ethical practices) that balance and support our contemplation of impermanence. 'Practice' is a whole life, not just individual techniques. What I mean by 'context' also entails a clear and helpful understanding of the teachings and where these are trying to point us. Lastly, as with any Buddhist practice, we will benefit from contemplating impermanence along with others, being able to share our experience, and receive guidance from someone more experienced who can show us the way, or guard against potential pitfalls. Therefore, what follows should be taken as a basic overview of a particular aspect of Buddhist practice, one that needs to take place within a broader supportive context.

We will look at three ways of contemplating impermanence. Together they consider change on three different 'timescales', or from three slightly different 'perspectives'. The first steps back and looks at our whole life in the light of impermanence, the second looks at how our day-to-day experience is always changing, and the third looks at change on a moment-by-moment basis.

The four reminders

The first approach is to look at our life, the opportunity it offers us, and the fact that it is fleeting and finite. Like many other religious and philosophical traditions, Buddhism encourages us to remember death, to think about it, to face the fact of our mortality. This is not intended to be morbid or frightening. It *is* meant to galvanize us, to give us a sense of urgency, energy, and motivation. In the affluent parts of our world, average life expectancy is about eighty years. That's 29,200 days, or 700,800 hours, or 42,048,000 minutes. How are we going to use them? Our life is of a limited span, so what is really important in our lives? What really matters and has priority? Let's not put off thinking about this until we are lying in that hospice bed; we can reflect on it now, and it can influence how we live our lives.

One example of a method for contemplating impermanence from this perspective is four sets of verses, known as the 'four preliminaries', from the Tibetan Buddhist tradition. The idea is to recite and reflect on these verses every day, perhaps first thing in the morning, or as part of our daily meditation practice. In the appendix to this book (see 'Reflection-meditation 1' on pp.196–200) is a version of the verses that you might like to make use of. Alternatively, you might find another version you prefer, or you might even write your own.[69]

Reflection time

The first verses deal with death, with the reality that we will one day die, reminding us that, though the time of death is unknown, the fact of death is certain. Those we love will die. Those we hate will die. In a hundred years almost everyone alive on the planet today will be gone. We are here for just a brief span of time.

The second set of verses tells us that, because life is fleeting, life is also precious; it is full of opportunity to cherish and appreciate rather than squander. This teaching is encouraging us to take a few moments to think of everything that we have received in our life and to reflect on the sheer wonder of existence, of being able to see, hear, touch, feel, think, and speak. We can also pause and recall parents, friends, teachers, and all those who have helped us. We can resolve to try and make the most of the opportunity our life offers.

In the third set of verses, we are asked to bring to mind ways in which life inevitably contains suffering. Even if our life now is happy and fortunate, there are many people in the world who are struggling, or leading wretched lives, sometimes of their own making, sometimes due to social or political forces. If we look at human history, and if we survey conditions of life across the globe, then it quickly becomes clear that, at the present time, we are living in a privileged era in history, and in a relatively affluent, stable, and peaceful region of the world. (I am assuming this is likely to be the case for most readers.)

The point of this reflection is not to make us feel guilty or gloomy, despondent or depressed, but, again, to remind us of the basic 'facts of life' and the need to practise Dharma (the Buddhist path and practices that help us move away from suffering and towards Enlightenment). So, fourthly, the last verses encourage us to remember that actions have consequences. We are making choices at every moment of our lives: through what we think, how we speak, and how we act. Those choices have an effect. They impact on the world and on other people, in small or large ways, for good or for ill.

And, crucially, they also impact on us and on the character we are constantly creating for ourselves. In Buddhism this is known as karma. Karma in this sense is not the punishment or reward of an outside agent; it is just how our thoughts shape our mind, which then shapes future experience. Through anything we do, say, or even think, we are creating particular tendencies, habits, or tracks in the mind, which shape our character, and therefore influence our future actions, words, and thoughts. The principle of karma describes how we are creating a moral personality for ourselves, at every moment of our lives, in everything that we think and do, large or small, positive or negative.

That character we develop influences our whole life; it colours the whole way we experience the world. For example, if I am kindly spoken, I tend to develop an easier going, more sympathetic, kinder personality. That means it becomes easier for me to speak kindly in the future. It also means that, quite likely, I will be popular and well liked and that people will return my kindness. Conversely, if I succumb to a habit of being rather acid-tongued, this tends to reinforce a mean and cynical attitude; whenever I speak there will be an inclination to harshness, and to see only the worst in people. To think and speak kindly becomes harder; it goes more against the grain, against force of habit. This may mean I am less popular and that fewer acts and words of kindness come my way in life. In this way, the principle of karma describes how ethical actions tend to produce happiness and unethical actions tend to produce unhappiness.

In daily life it often doesn't seem as clear as this; the dynamic of karma is not always so black and white, because not everything that happens to us is the result of karma. There are all sorts of conditions and influences at work in the world, and karma is only one amongst them. The kindly spoken person might still be mugged in the street, whereas the harshly spoken person might inherit a large sum. Nevertheless, it is likely that a kind-hearted person will be better able to bear their ordeal precisely because of that kindly attitude to life; it is also likely that the spiteful person won't find happiness through receiving a surprise windfall. So this fourth and last reflection is reminding us that everything we think and do is of significance. Just as even small drops of water will eventually fill a pot, we shouldn't underestimate the power of good or bad actions; even small thoughts, words, and acts have an effect on the kind of person we become.[70]

These four sets of verses are known as the 'four preliminaries' because they are traditionally reflected upon early on in the process of Dharma training, as a way of orientating and galvanizing the practitioner and instilling deeper in them the motivation to practise. For the same reason they are sometimes also referred to as the 'four thoughts that turn the mind towards the Dharma', or the 'four reminders'. We know life is fleeting, we know that worldly things can't give us lasting satisfaction, but we can forget and be swept along by them. These reflections are designed to help us remember, recalling the facts of life and death again and again so that they really sink in.

The essential purpose of reflecting in this way is to stay in more constant contact with what is really important and of true value in our life, not just letting life pass us by. If we kept the impermanent nature of our life in mind, then how might our priorities change? What would be seen in a different perspective? What different ethical choices might we make? As the Buddha says in the *Dhammapada*, those who remember death will compose their quarrels.[71] These reflections can be sobering, but they can also be energizing and freeing. It can even be a relief to finally face the truth of life simply and squarely.

How do we use these reflections? Perhaps we can recite them daily, as part of our meditation practice. We read them, slowly, just allowing the words and images to permeate our being. Once we are more familiar with them, we may be able to bring the reflections to mind on our own, without needing to read them. We bring to mind our own examples of what the words are referring to: loved ones who have passed away, the particular things in our life that we feel grateful for, and so on. We are not trying to force any emotional response. It is, to use a well-known analogy, like dropping pebbles into a still pool. We drop those words and phrases into the deep pool of our heart and pay attention to any ripples and resonances.

Like all the reflections in this chapter, context is crucial. For these teachings to bring lasting benefit, we need to understand, and have a degree of trust, that they are not just pointing out that life is hopeless and futile, but pointing to a deeper freedom and beauty that can be found through letting go. The reflections also need to be undertaken with loving-kindness. If you find yourself feeling low, or fearful, or confused and doubtful, then it could be best to put the reflections aside and practise loving-kindness. When you feel more emotionally buoyant, you can return to them again. In fact, contained within the four reminders is a kind of 'emotional balance' in that the first and the third confront us with the unwelcome reality of our situation, whereas the second and the fourth show us the positive potential of our life. The practice has, built into it, a balanced approach between challenging and undermining our complacency, and showing us how we can respond and keep initiative. We need to maintain that balance in our overall approach to practice. We need faith as well as wisdom.

One more thing that is good to bear in mind with the reflections in this chapter is that they can be applied to 'self' and 'other'. I don't just think of my impermanence, precious opportunity, suffering, and so on. I see that everyone is subject to these things. Again, it is important to maintain a balance, reflecting on our own life and also that of others.[72] Otherwise there is a danger that our reflection becomes subtly self-referential. Applying the reflection to both self and other, however, will help break down the distinction between them.

Sometimes this kind of reflection will feel like it is having a definite emotional impact. At other times, it feels like not much is happening, but we are nevertheless confident that we are turning our mind in a helpful direction. On other occasions it can feel that we are just repeating something in a rather formulaic fashion. Reflection does need to be repeated in order to go deeper; but it also needs to be kept fresh and relevant.

Yesterday, today, tomorrow

I have been using the 'four preliminaries' as an illustration of the first of three approaches to contemplating impermanence – the long view of impermanence, looking at our whole life in the light of its mortality. Sometimes, however, we need to consider impermanence nearer to us, to see the relevance of its teaching on a more day-to-day basis. This brings us to the second of those three approaches, which works in a very simple way. There is more detailed guidance for this in the appendix ('Reflection-meditation 2' on p.201); here I offer a basic outline. Sitting quietly, allowing the body and mind to settle and to begin to relax and open out a little, we recall the events of yesterday. Where were we yesterday, what did we do, what conversations did we have? How did our feelings and moods fluctuate through the day? Were there certain events that led us into craving or aversion? Do we remember particular stories and thought patterns that swirled around our mind? Can we recall pleasant or unpleasant sense experiences: the smell of roasting coffee in the café, or the cold wind and rain as we hurried to work? So much experience: where is it now?

We see that it has all gone, vanished forever. The events, feelings, sense experiences, and thoughts of yesterday have melted into thin air, dissolved into nothingness. And then we think about what today will bring. The day that lies ahead will involve new and unknown constellations of experiences, inner and outer. It, too, will depart as soon as it has arrived. What has seemed so real, important, or urgent today will, by tomorrow, be just memory, dreamlike and distant.

It is important to do this in a spirit of loving-kindness. We want to avoid an attitude of 'nihilism', thinking that, since nothing lasts, nothing can have any meaning or significance. Nor is it a case of 'dismissing' the experiences of yesterday, or subtly wanting to be rid of unwelcome experiences in an aversive way. This practice of looking through the lens of impermanence needs to be kept quite light and gentle. We just keep coming back to seeing how experiences come and go. This can help us release deep, habitual tendencies to 'bind to ourselves a joy', learning instead to 'kiss the joy as it flies'.

Of course experiences may arise today that are strongly influenced by what happened yesterday. For example, yesterday someone might have told us a piece of news, and its emotional impact has stayed with us. This way of reflecting is not denying connections between yesterday, today, and tomorrow. Rather, we are watching how one experience has come and gone and then, in dependence on that, another arises, and that too will fade away, and the process will continue.

This reflection may seem and feel very ordinary and unremarkable. In a way, it is! The point isn't to try and make 'something happen'. We keep observing the impermanence of things, we just keep observing again and again. We may notice this has an emotional effect; there might be a subtle sense of ease and equanimity. Something that I was irritated about yesterday now hardly seems to matter. Some pleasure that I am looking forward to is held with more lightness; we know it will just come and go. We are not *trying* to make ourselves feel a particular way; all we are trying to do is *look* at experience in a particular way, though it is good to notice any effect of this on our hearts and minds.

Impermanence moment by moment

The third approach to contemplating impermanence (see 'Reflection-meditation 3' in the appendix, pp.202–3) examines the transient nature of experience on an even more 'micro', momentary scale. As before, it requires the right conditions in order to be undertaken effectively. On the one hand, we need to be in a good enough state that our mind can be steady and focused, rather than being turbulent or agitated due to negative emotions. On the other hand, it doesn't need to be perfect; we don't have to postpone this kind of reflection until we have a wholly calm and concentrated mind. The reflection itself can actually provide interest, which then helps the mind to focus.

Our mind needs to be settled enough so that we are able to watch our experience arising and unfolding. We simply watch what happens, and we watch through the lens of impermanence; we notice how everything is always changing. Noises come and go. Body sensations – an itch, an ache, a judder of energy – come and go. Thoughts and images in the mind come and go. Some experiences come and go very quickly. Others linger for longer. Observing these carefully and with sensitivity, we may find that even they are subtly shifting and changing. At first, that ache in our shoulder feels solid and fixed, but now, looking more closely, we notice it throbs slightly, rising and falling in intensity, and shifting position. Perhaps we see how the quality of our attention influences our experience of that aching sensation. As we open to it, rather than tensing against it, it softens slightly, and feels less hard and rigid.

The main practice here is to observe change in our actual experience. It is not so much *thinking* about change as *experiencing* it directly, although that may of course involve some thought. Then you can also introduce another line of reflection: if all those experiences are changing, coming and going, then they can't really be 'mine' in an ultimate, absolute sense. I don't own them; I can't grasp hold of them and keep them. If their arising and ceasing are beyond my control, my conscious volition, then neither can they be 'me' in any final, absolute sense. Even inner feelings and thoughts that I tend to identify as 'me' just come and go, arise and cease, all the time. We try to neither identify with that flow of experience nor repulse and push it away. We just let there be a flow of experience, and we try to notice what that feels like.

As with the previous reflection, we need a background attitude of loving-kindness. Again, we may notice that contemplating in this way does have an effect on our mood and quality of awareness; there might be a subtle sense of lightness and equanimity, a kind of openness and expansiveness that comes from dis-identifying with elements of our experience in a limiting way. There might also be an increased sensitivity or aliveness to the subtleties of our experience: it becomes more of a melting flow than solid, fixed, discrete 'blocks' of experience. All this may well be quite subtle and gradual. Once again, it is important that we are not trying to make ourselves *feel* a particular way, but simply *looking* at experience in a particular way.

Our human bodies, for example, are continually changing. They take in food, water, warmth, and air from the surrounding environment. Solid and liquid matter is also ejected from the body, or is shed in the form of dead hair or skin, or sweat. Our bodies generate heat that then radiates away, and every inhalation of air is followed by exhalation and the return of gases into the atmosphere. Every cell in our bodies dies and is replenished in a seven-year cycle; seven years ago, none of the cells in our body existed. So who are we? From a certain point of view it makes sense to talk about 'my body'. But, looked at in another way, there is no 'body' that can ever be finally and fundamentally 'me' or 'mine'. There is borrowing and returning, receiving and releasing, growing and decaying, forming and dissolving. There is birth and death: this is what life is, and to try and stop the process, to try to seal and separate our bodies off from their surroundings would mean death in minutes. 'Body' is a process, not a fixed thing. Or you could say it is one temporary strand within a much larger process of life.

When we first reflect on 'not me' and 'not mine' this may seem a bit clunky and abstract, more an unfamiliar notion that we are applying to our experience, rather than a natural way of looking at and understanding what is going on. However, as with all the reflections we have been exploring, it will develop with practice. We are trying to *look* at our experience rather than think about it.

Perhaps we could even say that it is not so much a case of looking *at* experience, as if from the outside, but more a way of being *with* experience. This is something we gradually learn and then, through practice and repetition, it becomes a way of being we can adopt more quickly, easily, and naturally. It is like a perspective we can tune into, and, the more we have tuned into it in the past, the more we know the feel of what we are tuning into and where it will be found. An analogy for this could be that of learning to play a musical instrument. At first it is awkward and takes a lot of effort. With practice it comes more naturally, and a highly accomplished musician can just pick up the instrument any time and play with grace and ease, because the whole process has been learnt and internalized so thoroughly. Reflection and contemplation need this repetition to mature, to sink in deeper and become more natural to us.

Wise attention

Here we are trying to develop 'wise attention'. This is a translation of the term *yoniso manasikāra* from the early Buddhist tradition. *Yoniso* comes from the word *yoni*, which means 'womb' or 'place of origin'. So *yoniso* means getting to the bottom of things, beyond surface appearance. It also has the connotation of 'thorough' and 'wise', deep rather than superficial. *Manasikāra* means, quite literally, 'to do, or make, something in the mind'. It is usually translated as 'attention' or 'directionality of mind'. One of the necessary conditions of any moment of experience is that, knowingly or otherwise, we have directed our mind towards an object. If we direct our attention without awareness, craving or aversion may soon result. *Yoniso manasikāra*, by contrast, is 'wise attention', fully aware and ethically skilful.[73]

So we try to practise *wise* attention: not so much thinking *about* the Dharma, or even looking *at* the Dharma, but trying to look *with* the Dharma, to look through the lens of the Dharma at our experience, to look wisely. And it is also wise *attention*: to be efficacious, this way of looking requires a certain constancy of attention and focus. We need to be able to notice when our mind wanders and to come back to experience and looking with the Dharma. Otherwise, it is like trying to look at a cave painting with only a box of matches. We will get a quick glimpse, perhaps, only to be plunged back into darkness again. Then we catch another brief glimpse, but that too is gone before we can really see the whole picture. To really take it all in would require a steadier beam of light, such as from a candle or lamp. This is why Buddhist meditation emphasizes *samatha*, calming and concentrating the mind, so that the 'light' of our awareness and attention can be more steady and unwavering.

So far this chapter has been focused on ways of reflecting on impermanence whilst on our meditation seat or cushion. We need to learn to view our experience in this way whilst we are going about our daily life too. If a situation arises in which we are starting to grasp or repel, can we bring the Dharma to mind in that instant? Or, if not, can we come back to that incident later, and try to see it through more of a 'Dharma eye'?

In chapter 5, 'Healing time', I related the story of a friend of mine who struggled, and then succeeded, to forgive her parents for their violent treatment of her. A crucial aspect of this work of forgiveness was reflecting on impermanence. Again and again, my friend reminded herself that life was brief and fleeting, the time of death unknown. This motivated her to practise, to face the pain and anger so that these difficult emotions could be transformed. She didn't want either of her parents, or herself, to die before there was forgiveness. She saw how the 'characters' in the story that she told herself about her past didn't actually exist anymore. They were all gone, and in their place were different people. She saw the suffering that was perpetuated by holding on to fixed views of them. By looking at what was going on in her heart and mind through the lens of impermanence she was able, gradually, to undercut the fear and aversion that kept her locked inside an old and bitter story. Looking through that lens profoundly changed her attitude, leading to compassion for her parents.

This story illustrates how we can bring Dharma reflection to bear on the real issues of our life. The three reflections on impermanence described above are generalized practices that apply to anyone. They contain the essential principles and approach to practice. Then there is the creative and skilful application of those to the particular circumstances of our life, the specific ways we resist change or cling to the past, creating suffering for ourselves and others.

If we *apply* the Dharma, it matures within us, and slowly transforms us. If we don't use it, it remains on the level of

113

abstract ideas; those ideas may be interesting, even inspiring, but we are not actually changed by them. Reflecting on impermanence can have different effects on us. Sometimes it may feel exhilarating, galvanizing, and inspiring. For a few people it might provoke emotions of fear, in which case we need to emphasize kindness, and talk with others about what is going on. At other times the effect is quieter and more ordinary. But, if we look closely at our sense of self – look at the feeling-tone of the body, the quality of emotions and thoughts, the quality of our awareness – we may sense that these ways of looking have subtly changed us. Doing the 'yesterday and today' reflection, for example, I can feel a sense of the lightness of things, of how fleeting, ephemeral, temporary, and therefore provisional they are. This changes my feelings about them, and my attitude towards them. Things that might easily have swung my mood are now seen in a different, lighter perspective. Simultaneously, and perhaps paradoxically, time also becomes more rich and precious; each moment matters. Every single day has meaning and significance in the overall story of our lives. Time – and life – becomes lighter and more ephemeral, but also more potent; it becomes deep as well as constantly flowing. Like a dancer leaping and landing, time is light, agile, fast-moving, but also full of expressive presence.

Another effect of reflecting on impermanence is that it can make death seem more natural, part of life, less surprising and frightening. It is not that I wouldn't be shocked and upset if someone I loved died suddenly and unexpectedly. But there would also, I hope, be another part of me that would know this can happen; that its possibility is woven into the fabric of life. Eventually that knowing, that familiarity, gained through regular reflection on impermanence, would have an effect, helping me to accept and understand my loss, and to be able to grieve and start to come to terms with it.

Reflection time

We think we know about impermanence; it is obvious that things change. Yet to really, fully understand requires that we look more deeply, right into the mystery of it. We think we already know that 'things change', but we start to see that there is a never-ending process of change that manifests each moment as particular experiences and phenomena. Every 'thing' is an in-between, a momentary constellation between what it just came from and what it will soon become, a suspension between immediate past and immediate future. Nothing exists in an absolute or enduring sense; it is all *śūnya* – empty of fixed and inherent existence – to use the Buddhist terminology. And that means there really is nothing we can grasp hold of.

Looking deeper into impermanence, we see the wide-open-yet-particular, everything-and-nothing, ephemeral-yet-vivid, ungraspable and mysterious nature of things. This is not to deny the fullness and richness of our experience. It is just that we are so liable to mistake the nature of that experience; it doesn't exist as fixed, separate, enduring things. Our categories of 'existence' and 'non-existence' are too clumsy. The reality is a more subtle in-between, such that in Buddhist cultures it has often been described as illusory, like a conjuring trick, appearing and disappearing out of thin air.

The real point of this 'wise attention' is to set us free from our grasping and repelling of life. This will also set us free from self-reference and self-clinging, so that we are more able to respond to life, and to other people, with awareness, kindness, and compassion. Our life bears fruit out of a dynamic between two seemingly contradictory movements. One is a move away from the world, letting go, or giving up. Realizing that the world cannot offer certainty or permanence may lead us to withdraw our energy and emotional investment from certain activities. But Buddhist practice doesn't entail only that withdrawal. It is also a reinvestment, and engagement with the world and other people. These two 'movements' are expressed mythically in the Buddha's life story; he retreats into the forest to meditate and seek Enlightenment, but then he returns to the towns and cities to help and teach others. Both of these movements – away from and towards the world – are essential to the point and purpose of the Buddha's teaching.

9 o'clock

Self and time

Many writers and thinkers have noted the difficulty of defining time, perhaps most famously Saint Augustine, the fifth-century philosopher and theologian who wrote in his *Confessions*: 'If no one asks me, I know; but if any person should require me to tell him, I cannot.'[74] Time is such an intrinsic part of our experience, so threaded in to how we go about living our life. Yet it is very hard to say exactly what it is, or how it works.

We certainly seem to have a strong sense of time. We perceive things in the world around us beginning, enduring for a while, and then coming to an end. Some things last for what seems like a short time, other things for longer; in other words, we can compare their duration. We also place events in a temporal order; we know that *this* thing happened before *that* one; we know that, for example, to bake a cake you mix up all the ingredients *before* you put them in the oven. We can plan and anticipate the future and, in order to do so, we call upon what we have learnt and experienced in the past. Our minds work temporally, able to constantly rewind to the past or zip forward to the future. We instinctively and immediately intuit, when a thought or sensation comes into awareness, whether it is a memory from the past, a new experience in the present, or an idea or fantasy about the future. We just *know*, quite automatically, without any conscious thinking or effort on our part, where (or rather when) it belongs in the temporal order.

Time seems so real, obvious, normal, and part of everyday experience. And yet it is so hard and elusive to define. With space we can wave our arms around us and say: 'Here it is; this is it!' It appears to be more directly and straightforwardly 'there'. It is harder to pin down time, to point it out, to get hold of it, to show it to someone. Its very nature is to constantly slip through our fingers and disappear. As discussed in chapter 6, our language for time is metaphorical; we constantly use *spatial* metaphors to talk about time, rather than talking about it directly. The past is 'behind' us, the future is 'over the horizon'.[75] Time goes round in circles or along a line (as in 'timeline' or 'lineage').[76] Time can 'stand still' or it can 'race ahead'.

We say: 'Thankfully his speech was over *in* one hour.' In this way of speaking, time is a space in which the speech took place. Or we say: 'Three hours *passed* before she stopped talking.' The verb 'to pass' has the same root as 'to pace'; both come from the Latin *passus*, which means 'a stretch of the leg'. Or: 'We *endured* his terrible violin playing for two hours.' 'Endure' derives from a root that means 'to harden'. 'It *took* five hours to arrive at the concert': 'to take' is to get, capture, grasp, or lay hold of. 'The speech was dull; I *lasted* only half an hour before falling asleep': 'to last' means to afford or yield. These are all spatial metaphors. It seems impossible to talk about time directly.

Chapter 6 also investigated how everything we experience is in a process of flux. We experience change, we compare different processes of change, and we call this 'time'. The very way in which we experience change is by thinking it happened in time, or that time went by as it happened. How we perceive change, and use language to describe it, relies on this notion of time, which, on close inspection, is highly metaphorical. In other words, we experience change and time in a particular way because our minds work in a particular way. This chapter examines more closely this subject-dependent, mind-dependent aspect of time.

Time in the mind

There is a puzzle or conundrum, often quoted in philosophy textbooks, in which we are asked to imagine a tree falling in a forest. The forest is far from any humans, and there are no animals present to witness the event either. The question posed is: when the tree falls, does it make a sound?

Our gut response can be to say: 'Yes, of course the tree would come crashing down and make a huge sound.' But on further reflection we realize that this is not the case at all. It may be that the fall of the tree agitates the molecules of air around it, and those vibrations may set off other air molecules for some distance around. However, vibrations of air aren't sound. For there to be sound, the disturbance of the air molecules would need to be at the right amplitude and frequency to stimulate an eardrum, in order to activate nerves and send a message along neural pathways in the brain, and for this to then be experienced as sound in someone's (or some creature's) awareness. Even the greatest tree in the forest makes no sound when it comes toppling down. If there is no one there observing and perceiving, it falls completely silently. For there to be a sound there has to be an observer, or perceiver; there needs to be someone, or something, doing the experiencing.

It is the same with the colour of the tree. If it is a spruce tree, for example, then we might believe that the needles will be dark blue-green. Yet, in itself, a leaf on the tree has no colour. For there to be colour, a whole range of other conditions need to be present. Light needs to hit the leaves and then, whilst they will absorb light of some frequencies, they will reflect light from other parts of the spectrum. Some of that reflected light then needs to register on the retina of an observer, be processed in the brain, and create a sensation of colour. And similarly with smell: the spruce tree may secrete a resin, but this in itself has no aroma, unless some of those chemicals register on the olfactory cells of a perceiver and are turned into the experience and awareness of smell.

Sound, colour, smell (and other qualities like taste or texture) are real experiences that we have, and yet they don't abide in individual objects themselves. They are subject-dependent. They are not entirely subjective: two or more observers with similar sense faculties and cognitive faculties tend to report similar experiences of the sound a falling tree makes, or the colour or smell of a spruce. (Of course I can never know what someone else actually experiences when they tell me they see 'blue-green'. I do not know if it is the same as what goes on in my experience. Nevertheless, we do both agree that the needles on the spruce tree are a particular colour, distinct from the shade of green of beech or oak leaves.)

Not entirely objective, not entirely subjective: all experience arises out of this interaction of 'perceiver' and 'perceived'. Experience *is* that interaction. We can never know the world fully objectively; whatever the tree (or anything else in the world) is *in itself* is beyond our knowing. So what has all this got to do with time? I want to give this old philosophical conundrum a temporal twist and ask: if a tree falls in the forest and there is no one for miles around to witness the event, *at what time* does the tree fall?

If there is no one there to experience, there can't be a *now*. 'Now' is subjective, perspectival. Now is where and when you are or I am; now is the moment from which we witness events unfolding. And if, without an observer, there can't be a now, then there can't be a past or a future either, because they only exist relative to the present. So who can say what time the tree fell?[77]

Someone might reply that we could leave a timer and video camera running in the forest with no one present, so that later we would be able to watch the film and know exactly when the tree fell. Such knowledge, though, is still only in relation to a knower, a subject, the person watching the film, and therefore in relation to their 'now'. The 'when' of its falling is still, in some way, subject-dependent. A stronger argument would be that there must be an objective time the tree fell, because on investigation we find that it fell *after* very strong winds that came *after* a great rainstorm that washed soil off the bank where the tree fell. We deduce the *cause* of the tree falling and that events must have happened in a particular *order*. If there is an order to events, then surely that means they happen at a certain time?

Even if those events did happen, independently of an observer, and even if they happened in a particular sequence, that sequence, or order, isn't the same as time. There is still something about time that is subject-dependent. Without an observer, there cannot be a 'now', and without a 'now' there cannot be past or future. There is something about time, or at least about 'tensed time' (past, present, future) that is mind-dependent, that is constructed by the perceiving subject.[78]

In a similar fashion, it makes no sense to say the tree fell 'forwards'. In itself, the tree has no 'forwards'. Only if we imagined ourselves standing in the tree's place would 'forwards' or 'backwards' mean anything. In other words, they are perspectival, subject-dependent. Living in England, I think America is 'west' and Russia is 'east'. That is also how they are represented on a map or atlas. But that is only a cartographical convention. If I travelled from England to Alaska, most of America would now be 'east' and Russia would be 'west'. There is no absolute 'east' or 'west'; they only have meaning in relation to a perceiving subject. Similarly there is no absolute 'now', 'earlier', or 'later'; they exist only relative to an experiencing subject (or subjects).

In chapter 1 ('Flexi time'), we investigated how our experience of time is conditioned by our state of mind, particularly how our perception of time is stretched or contracted by states of craving or aversion. In chapter 4 ('Story time'), we examined how we constantly narrate our life: we interpret, we tell ourselves a story, and these stories then become the 'frameworks' by which we comprehend new situations that we encounter. Frameworks from our past determine what it is possible for us to perceive (or not perceive) in the future. However, what we are now considering is how time is mind-made even more fundamentally. We are seeing, on an even deeper level, how our mind imposes a framework on reality in order to make sense of it, in order to turn it into experience. Tensed time is one of the most base-level frameworks that we apply. It is not that we experience things in time, but that time is how we experience things. Consciousness is not in time; it is nearer the truth to say that time is in consciousness. Time and space are what the philosopher Immanuel Kant called 'forms of intuition': they are how our mind structures and orders experience, they are how we *have* experience.

Contemporary British philosopher Bryan Magee has likened this to the way in which a camera must take pictures, rather than make a sound recording. To a camera (if it were sentient!), experience would *have* to appear visually, rather than audibly, because that is the nature of a camera.[79] In a similar way, our sense faculties and the nature of our mind mean that experience *has* to take given forms – particular types of sense impression organized temporally and spatially. We can't even begin to envisage experience being any other way; we simply don't have the faculties for that. For example, we can never really know what it is like to be a bat dashing round trees and houses in the black of night, snapping up tiny flies, navigating solely by echolocation. We can try to envisage what kind of experience this would be, but we can only do so in terms of the sense faculties that we humans have – for example, by imagining that the bat builds up a 'picture' from the rebounding sounds. What the bat is doing, however, is outside the possibility of our experience.

It is deeply counterintuitive to accept that the world doesn't really exist, independently and separately from us, exactly as our mind represents it. Seeing is believing: it seems so obvious that what we see (or hear, smell, taste, or touch) exists in a world out there, in precisely the way that it appears to us. Similarly with time; it is very difficult to really take on the idea that the flow of time and the sense of 'now' isn't how the world is in itself, and that it is just a form, or framework, that we are imposing on reality. Our assumption of realism, that reality is exactly like our minds' representations of it, is deeply instinctual.

This temporal framework, embedded into the way our human mind works, might be partly explained by taking an evolutionary perspective. That sense of being here in the 'present' and having a conception of 'future' would allow an early human being to have a sense of agency and to plan ahead. Complex learning requires memorization and, in a given situation, being able to recall what worked last time round; in other words, it requires an idea of the past. For example, being aware that a herd of animals you are hunting, although not perceived now, were seen yesterday drinking at that river at sundown, and will therefore most likely come back at sundown, again necessitates the organization of experience into past, present, future. All this requires that a dynamic sense of time, flowing from future into present into past, be part of one's cognitive apparatus.[80]

Animals certainly undertake different activities at particular times; there are times in the day for eating or sleeping, times in the year for mating and nesting, hibernating or migrating. These behaviours, however, are more instinctual and habitual; it is not that the animal has self-consciously estimated time and believes that 'now' is the right time to do them. Of course some animals do have memory. A dog, for example, can remember and differentiate between the person who kicked him last week and the person who offered kindness and affection. Even so, although the dog can perceive someone approaching and know whether to growl or wag its tail, this is more of an instinctual response that arises in the moment. The dog can't dwell in the past to nearly the same extent that a human can; it probably doesn't lie awake at night mulling over what happened last week, or fantasizing about an ideal future. Animal consciousness is more strongly located in present experience, whereas human consciousness can move more flexibly between yesterday, today, and tomorrow.[81]

How time and self are interrelated

To summarize the ground covered so far in this chapter: human beings have a very strong sense of time – it is an intrinsic part of our experience; it seems so real, natural, obvious, and self-evident. But if we investigate that experience more closely, and if we analyze our notions of time, it becomes more elusive – we can't find it. Time, or at least time tensed into past, present, and future, seems rather a way in which we *have* experience, a mode of being in which reflective awareness of a world is made possible.

Does this remind you of some other entity that is much discussed in Buddhism? A central, core teaching of the Buddha was that of *anātman*, usually translated as 'no self' or 'no fixed self'. This is a similarly counterintuitive notion: surely we must have a self? Don't we *feel* a sense of self, sometimes so vividly and urgently? Here we are in our physical bodies experiencing sensations that feel pleasant or painful, and being motivated to act in order to seek one and avoid the other. The experience of 'me' feels so real and yet, when we try to find the self through meditative introspection, we find only sensations, feelings, thoughts, volitions. We find a stream of activities and experiences in the mind, but we don't find the activator or experiencer.

Self and time

Like time, the self isn't a 'thing'. It is *how* we have experience; it is the way our mind has developed for presenting experience: it presents it from 'out there' in the world to a me 'in here'. Again, like time-awareness, we could give an explanation of human self-awareness in terms of its evolutionary advantages. It is very difficult, if not impossible, for us to imagine human beings doing without this notion of real existing entities that are 'me' and 'you'. For starters it would make communication very tricky. Try arranging a meeting with a friend, a trip to the cinema perhaps, without referring to 'I' or 'you'. See if you can agree which film to watch and whether you both make it to the cinema at the right time!

The Buddha wasn't concerned about *anātman* for abstract, theoretical reasons. For him, the roots of human happiness or suffering were found through understanding the true nature of the human self. I am going to suggest a reflection, or thought experiment, to help us investigate further.

You will find more detailed instructions for this reflection in the appendix ('Reflection-meditation 4', p.204), but the gist of the exercise is to recall different situations that you have found yourself in, and to try and connect with, to feel, what your 'sense of self' was like in those moments. What did it feel like to be 'you'? How did it feel physically, in the body? How did it feel emotionally, in the heart? How did it feel mentally; what was the tone and type of thinking that occurred in that situation? In this exercise, we reflect on our experience of self, or sense of self, in three different types of scenario: firstly, where we were irritated, or stressed, or defensive in some way; secondly, where we were generous, or kind, or content in some way, large or small; and then, lastly, a time when we were at our very best, perhaps a situation in which we were deeply content, or inspired, or creative, or maybe an activity in which we were totally absorbed or engaged.

Free Time!

The following paragraphs outline what people tend to report when they do this exercise. If you would like to do it yourself, it is probably best not to read on till after you have completed it, so that you can approach it free of expectations.

Describing how they feel in themselves when irritated, anxious, or defensive (the first scenario), people use words like: separate, isolated, small, tight, constricted, narrow, inflexible, circular thoughts, disintegrated, jangled, unconnected, or short-sighted. When describing their experience of themselves when generous, friendly, or kind (the second scenario), people often call on words such as: light, expansive, connected, alive, adaptable, flowing, whole, integrated, sensitive, empathic, spacious, or joyful. Trying to describe how we feel in ourselves in situations of being at our very best and most inspired might be a bit harder, partly because it may be more of an occasional experience, or one that took place longer ago. Nevertheless, some people will say that it is like an even more energized, flowing, and expansive version of the second experience. They also use words like: complete, compassionate, timeless, potent, responsive, purposeful, effortless, totally present. There can also be something that is harder to put into words; whilst there may be tremendous energy and purpose, there is somehow less sense of ego driving it, or being at the centre of it all.

That is, there is usually a 'sense of self', a sense of what it feels like to be 'me'. We interpret the 'feel' of our body, mind, and heart, the feel of the particular sensations, thoughts, and volitions that are occurring at any moment, as being 'me'. In this way, we feel a sense of self. But that sense of self is always changing; it is being constructed, created, and recreated every moment of our days.[82] Thoughts or acts that are underlain by craving or aversion tend to create or perpetuate a sense of self that feels more fixed and definite, more separate and hard-edged. This can then become 'self-perpetuating'; feeling defensive or inadequate is likely to lead to more craving and aversion, which reinforce and refabricate the same brittle, inwardly turned sense of self. Thoughts or acts of generosity or kindness, conversely, create a sense of self that is more open, expansive, outwardly turned, connected, and flexible. We become less self-centred. To forget ourselves, to be more selfless, gives relief and creates freedom.

How we think, speak, and act creates and recreates our sense of self, every minute of every day. Some volitions and perceptions (emotions and thoughts) are repeated; they become habits, and so our very sense of self becomes partly automatic and habitual. That means the sense of self, the feeling of 'me' that those attitudes and actions create, is also recreated again and again. It therefore appears to be more constant and consistent, and so *appears* to be a stable, enduring entity, rather than an experience that has been created in our mind. But as the Pali scholar Andrew Olendzki has written:

> [G]rasping isn't something done by the self; rather, self is something done by grasping.[83]

If we reify those ever changing processes that are our experience into an absolutely real and unchanging self, then we are bound to want to protect and maintain this self. We compare it with other selves; we worry about whether we are better, worse, or the same as them. And, because that fixed, solid self is not actually there, there is always something about it that feels elusive and empty; we respond to that feeling by restlessly, endlessly searching for fulfilment. All this creates emotional suffering and existential angst. And there is no end to it. No end, that is, unless there is some degree of insight into the provisional and contingent nature of the self – which is what the Buddha was advocating.

Sometimes, understandably, people can find the teaching of 'no self' confusing. Maybe the words can be misleading. The language of 'no self' can make it sound like all the experiences that people were describing in that earlier exercise are being denied.

Saying self is unreal can seem like saying the experience of being 'me' is also illusory and non-existent. Those experiences, however, are real experiences. There *is* a changing flow of experience; but there isn't a fixed entity behind them.

Perhaps the language of 'no self' can also lead us into thinking we must try and 'get rid' of the self. But we can't do that, in the sense that we can't just stop how our mind functions and presents experience to us. That first-person perspective – the way mind presents experience from 'out there' to 'me in here' – isn't itself the problem. That 'perspectival self' will be present whenever we are having experience. The problem is interpreting this process of mind into a fixed thing, and then falling into grasping and repelling in order to defend and enhance it. We can, however, learn not to reify it into a really existing entity; we can understand and relate to it as more provisional and contingent. We see the nature of mind and self for what they really are. We can also try to think and act in ways that we know will bring about a happier and freer sense of self. Being generous and acting for the benefit of others, rather than solely out of self-interest, or in pursuit of our own preferences and desires, are practical ways in which we can act on this insight and take self less seriously. Perhaps, sometimes, when we do this, we will have experiences of that first-person self feeling much lighter and more diaphanous, or more free and expansive, or even becoming extremely subtle, refined, and pure.

An Enlightened being never becomes attached to an idea of self, never clings to any particular state or experience, saying: 'that's *me*, that's *mine*'. The third part of the reflection exercise was hinting at what the Enlightened experience might be like. The practice of ethics (kindness, generosity, truthfulness) moves us from the experience of self as more small, fixed, and separate (the first part of the exercise) to a sense of self that is increasingly expansive, fluid, and connected (the second part of the exercise).

If we keep orienting practice and awareness in that direction, and if we also keep remembering the conditioned, fabricated nature of self, this makes it more possible and likely that the third way of being can arise.

The Buddha therefore described the practice of ethics and wisdom as like two hands washing each other, each one cleansing and purifying the other. He described this combination of ethics and wisdom as the 'highest thing in the world'.[84] Ethics creates that more open and expanded sense of self, which will tend to be less rigid and defended, and therefore more receptive and sensitive to the truth. Wisdom then sees that even this relatively refined self is contingent, ever changing, and therefore not to be attached to. This can then motivate even deeper, more selfless, ethical practice. And this, in turn, creates a self that is able to manifest an even more wise perspective. In this way, ethics and wisdom deepen each other and free us from suffering.

I have noted that craving and aversion produce a tighter, smaller, harder knot of self, but *how* do they do that? If we really want something (craving), or we don't want it (aversion), then the mind tends to become extremely involved with thinking about that thing. It is as if the mind obsesses, revolves around that object in tight circles, exaggerating the pleasant features of the craved object, or the unpleasant features of the hated object. Such mental activity makes that object loom large in our mind, makes it more than it really is. The sense of disparity between 'me' and the object becomes heightened; it increases the sense of polarization between them, creating that stronger, more burning sense of 'self'. This further reinforces the deluded tendency to imagine that self to be a real entity. It is a misinterpretation that is innately, but not inescapably, human. In that sense it is an entirely understandable misinterpretation. Nevertheless, according to the Buddha, it limits human freedom and potential.

Freeing time and freeing self

We have been exploring similarities between our time-sense and self-sense, and how both of them are constructed in the mind. These similarities aren't merely coincidental. Time and self are deeply and fundamentally connected, mutually dependent. Self is the imagined fixed point of reference that enables us to have a temporal perspective. Time is the flow of events past that fixed point of self. (Or it is an imagined line along which the self travels.) When, through craving and aversion, our self-sense is more contracted and inflexible, our sense of time will also be more tense, more hard and pressing. When our sense of time is more urgent, when we are trying to grasp or fight time, then our sense of self will also be more tightly wound up.

My experience might feel pleasant, and so I crave more of that pleasure and am averse to any changed future state. (In other words, I am resisting change.) This means my mind will tend to grasp the object that is perceived as giving pleasure, and push away from what I identify as bringing change. This creates a more polarized sense of 'self' and 'other', and also of 'now' and 'then'. The feeling of self becomes heightened, as does the feel of the gap between present and future. This is then experienced as a faster subjective experience of time; the future state that we don't want feels like it comes up quicker. All this will, in turn, tend to reinforce clinging and holding on.

Alternatively, my experience might feel unpleasant, and so I am pushing it away and longing for a different experience. (In other words, I am craving change.) My mind grasps onto its image or idea of that desired future state, and becomes intensely focused on the gap between it and me. It is like the mind is now straining forwards. This, again, accentuates the sense of 'me' as I am 'now' and 'me' as I would be 'then'. In this way, along with the self-sense, the time-sense is also more urgent, although in this instance it makes the gap between present and future seem longer. I am *here*, but I want to be *there*; this creates a slower subjective experience of time, which again reinforces the desire and longing.[85]

If, however, we are content, free of craving and aversion, this lessens and relaxes the sense of self. There is little or no clinging to the present, or longing for the future, no urge to stay or go. This means less intense and loaded fabrication in the mind of 'now' and 'then', less urgency and polarization between present and future. Our subjective experience of time will therefore be more relaxed. This will enable us to tune in to the time of another person, to synchronize with their need to talk slowly, or move quickly. We can dance with them, fall into step with their rhythm; we can make time for them.

If we look forward to something happening, time slows; if we don't want it to happen, it comes up more quickly! Why does our mind produce a sensation of time that is the *opposite* of what we actually want? One answer would be that it is the mind's trick for getting us to focus and act more strongly; the mind presents us with a heightened, and more time-pressured, experience of what we do or don't want, so that we are galvanized to push or pull from it with even more determination.

This still doesn't fully explain how craving change (or aversion to present experience) seems to *slow* time, whereas craving continuity (or aversion to change) seems to *speed up* time. Here is an image that might help. Imagine two trains on parallel tracks, running along side by side. You are on one train, looking out of the window at the other. The one train is 'you'; the other train is the 'world' that you look out on, the world that you experience.

For a while the two trains are running along, side by side, at exactly the same speed. You look at the other train, and it appears not to be moving. You can quite clearly see the passengers on the other train. If you glance out of the opposite window at the landscape, you get a sudden, strange, sensation of moving again. Then you look back at the other train and everything seems more still.

This is an analogy for awareness and attention being perfectly in the flow of time, not craving past or future. You move forwards and yet, simultaneously, there is a great clarity, almost a stillness, to your experience. Recently I met an accomplished jazz musician and I asked him about his experience of time when playing music. 'It is wonderful,' he said, 'it is totally timeless.' 'But,' I replied, 'aren't you keeping time, keeping perfect rhythm, with the other musicians? How can that be timeless?' His response was that these were two different things. The musicians could be highly aware of each other, in synch with each other. In that sense, they kept perfect time. But that perfect time, being in total harmony with each other, then felt 'timeless'. The two trains running alongside each other, and you on one train, watching the other, which seems to both move and not-move, are an image of this 'timelessness'.

Next, imagine that your train is accelerating, pulling forwards. This represents your mind's attention straining ahead, in anticipation or longing of the future. Now, as you look at the other train, it appears to be going slower; it may even seem to go backwards. You can no longer see it so clearly; the passengers on the other train are just a blur. Our awareness and attention are no longer flowing along in harmony with things, but urging forwards, and so things appear to move slower.

Finally, imagine that now your train is braking, holding back. This represents your mind resisting the future and pushing away from it. Suddenly the other train seems to be hurtling forwards, and again, it is hard to see the other people so clearly. Once more, there is a bias in our awareness, our attention is loaded a particular way, and this produces a distorted experience of time.[86]

When, in the story told in chapter 1, the student took the Zen master to the airport, she was desperately craving for the bus to turn up on time. Perhaps all sorts of forces were at work:

wanting to be liked by her teacher, fearing his disapproval, or anger and irritation at the bus company. Time felt tight, which triggered craving and aversion, and this then wound time tighter still. The Zen master, however, didn't identify so strongly with catching or not catching the plane, and so didn't allow thoughts of grasping or repelling to proliferate in his mind. Self was more easy and expansive, and so time, too, stayed smooth and spacious. Craving and aversion, self, and time are intimately related and interconnected.

Buddhist tradition encourages us to see through our reification of the self, to unpack and open out the structure of experience, so that our whole life can be more expansive, and free. Living ethically, broadening and deepening awareness through meditation, and seeing deeply into how the mind fabricates experience are all crucial to this process. Another possible approach could be to reflect deeply and closely on our experience of time. Gradually we can move away from relating to time as something fixed, external, and separate from us, and rather see it as part of the structure of awareness. Through this process, we can move from 'tensed time' to 'free time'. Our sense of time can unfold, feeling less taut, knotted, and conflicted, and more relaxed and harmonious. Perhaps we will have glimpses of a timelessness that seems peaceful and beautiful.

10 o'clock

Now time

Read popular contemporary books on Buddhism, or on mindfulness, or other books of Buddhist-inspired 'spirituality', and the idea of 'being in the now' crops up again and again. The reader is exhorted to 'be here now'; we're told that 'only the present moment is real'. Closely related to this emphasis are other ideas and attitudes: the desirability of 'acceptance', scepticism about the need for effort or striving, and suspicion about conceiving of the Buddhist life in any future-orientated way, such as thinking of it in terms of 'development' or 'evolution'.

This is curious because, if we read the early Buddhist scriptures, which are as close as we can get to the actual words of the historical Buddha, we find that he never used such language. The Buddha didn't express himself in that way; he didn't tell his followers that 'it is only ever now' or that 'the present is the only place you can be'.[87] He did, however, frequently talk about the need for energy, effort, and striving. His last words are reputed to have been *appamādena sampādetha*, often translated as: 'with mindfulness strive on'.

This contrast of messages is a consequence of the tradition of Buddhism meeting the conditions and concerns of people in a very different twenty-first-century world, and of those traditional Buddhist teachings being understood and then articulated in a very particular manner. Does this represent a skilful re-expression of timeless truths in a way that is helpful to modern human beings? Or is there a subtle distortion of the original message of the Buddha? These questions are the basis for this chapter. They are inseparable from the further question of what constitutes a healthy and happy relationship to past, present, and future.

Motivating the current advocacy of 'being in the present moment' are various overlapping concerns and preoccupations that are to do with the conditions that we moderns find ourselves living in, our daily struggles, how *dukkha* (unsatisfactoriness) manifests in our twenty-first-century lives. We live in a culture that can be highly individualistic and driven, busy and hectic, full of constant input and stimulation. So much of our world is fast-changing, always hurtling into a brand new future. As we shall see, our longing to 'be in the moment' is, in large part, a tactical response, a survival mechanism, a bid for sanity in the helter-skelter world we live in.

I have taught probably hundreds of introductory meditation classes over the years and, when I have asked people why they want to meditate, they have frequently replied: 'I just want to switch off.' Given the stresses and strains of many people's lives, this is entirely understandable. But 'switching off' isn't what the Buddha taught. Of course we need to relax. Many people are obliged to manage extremely demanding jobs, perhaps dealing with impossible budgets and targets, or conflict and antagonism, or seeing close up the suffering that blights others' lives. When they arrive home at the end of the day, they need to unwind. 'With mindfulness strive on' probably doesn't sound so appealing when we are exhausted after a heavy day at the office. By contrast, that peaceful, gently smiling image of the Buddha, sitting serenely in meditation, may appear very alluring, may look just like what we need.

So Buddhism is interpreted and taken up in a culturally conditioned and culturally specific manner. Ideas such as 'stopping thoughts', 'switching off', 'staying in the present', or 'simply being' feel relevant and attractive. And this is fine as far as it goes, as long as we don't turn such ideas into the whole of what Buddhism offers. The danger of going unawares too far down this road is that we limit our understanding of Buddhism, turning it into an escape from the hurly-burly of the real world, rather than seeing it as a movement of spiritual and social transformation.

Proliferating thoughts and the value of the present moment

Of course we can't know for sure how people in other times and cultures experienced life, but it does seem that ours is a particularly 'heady' culture. We can have a strong tendency to be lost in fantasy, distraction, worry, to be caught up in thoughts that spin dizzyingly round inside our heads. We are told that anxiety and depression are endemic in the contemporary world, causing huge suffering; a key component of both of these is unhelpful, highly subjective, and relentless rumination.

In a teaching rather quaintly known as 'the honeyball'[88] the Buddha explained how, when experiencing pleasant or unpleasant feelings, our thinking minds can go into overdrive, fuelled by craving and aversion towards those feelings. He called such thinking *papañca*, often rendered as 'proliferation'. We think endlessly about the person we have fallen in love with, and our thinking exaggerates their pleasant features and creates lovely, romantic images of togetherness with them. Or we fume repeatedly about the person who irritates us, and our mental picture of them becomes distorted, their negative qualities writ large, their positive qualities hardly visible at all.

The result, said the Buddha, is that we end up living in our heads, and in a kind of fantasy world. That world may seem pleasant (the romantic dream) or unpleasant (the angry, self-righteous viewpoint) but, either way, it is going to lead us into trouble because it is imaginary. The antidote is to try not to engage in this mental proliferation, but to stay with our direct experience. What is really happening? How does it make us feel? What are those feelings of pleasure or pain really like? What emotions are at work, pushing us into reacting to those feelings?

Papañca consists of mental fantasy or worry about the past or future, whereas the practice of mindfulness seeks to return us to our experience, here, now, in the present. Directing our attention and awareness into the physical body can help to start this process. Only from that awareness of our actual experience can we gain perspective and stop perpetuating unhelpful thoughts and emotions. Putting it another way, we tend to react to the 'primary reality' (what is actually happening), thereby constructing a 'secondary reality' (the fantasy in our heads that will be, at best, only partially true). It is, however, possible to disengage from the secondary reality by bringing awareness to our primary reality again. (Primary reality is constructed too. But, for now, we are concerned with dropping a highly constructed and artificial reality for one that is 'less constructed' and that is relatively true and helpful.)

Although the Buddha himself didn't use such a form of words in the honeyball teaching, we can still see how that teaching leads into the language of 'being in the now'. We can appreciate how it makes sense to say that, if we are to deal with *papañca*, then the present is where we need to be, not the past or the future. For us right now, the past and future don't exist, except as mental proliferation in our heads. Thinking about past and future creates *dukkha*; it is better to drop them and to stay in the present moment.

So 'being in the present moment' can be a very helpful and practical idea to work with. However, this technique for calming the mind is not the ultimate goal of practice. It is what Buddhist tradition might call a 'skilful means'; it is a way of getting us so far, which is good and necessary, as long as we don't mistake 'so far' for the real point and purpose of the Buddhist path. The freedom the Buddha was trying to point people towards went much deeper than 'staying in the now'. The idea of a 'now' only exists relative to the idea of past and future. If we have a notion of a 'now' that we need to 'stay in', then that implies a notion of past and future that we need to 'stay out of'. In other words, we are still living boxed in by mind-created time. There will remain, if only very subtly, an attachment to 'now' and an aversion to 'past' or 'future'.

Finding a moment

A moment of sound or a thought arises into the light of awareness and then recedes into darkness again. As soon as we notice the experience, it has disappeared into the past. We can recall that moment of experience, but what we recall isn't the experience itself, only memory. As far as I am concerned, the actual experience no longer exists; it isn't still sitting there in some place called 'the past'. There is no past, only passed.

Nor, for me right now, does the future exist. We may have predictions, assumptions, or hopes about the future, but these are not the future itself, only ideas and thoughts that are occurring in the present, before immediately slipping away into the past again.

Yet the present moment: surely *that* exists and is real? Major figures in the Buddhist tradition, especially practitioners from the Perfection of Wisdom school such as Nagarjuna, deconstructed even our notions of the 'moment'.[89] To explore what this might mean, we can watch and examine the 'present moment' in our own experience.[90] There is more guidance for how to do this in the appendix (see 'Reflection-meditation 5', pp.205–6). What follows now is a brief explanation of the method, followed by a discussion of what you may discover – though you need to look and decide for yourself! We need to sit quietly and allow the mind to settle somewhat. We try to 'step back' so as to watch our own mind at work, see experiences as they arise and fall in awareness, but without becoming drawn into them and distracted, or pushing them away and avoiding them. At the same time, we allow ourselves to experience them; it is not some kind of removed and aloof awareness that we are trying to cultivate. This is quite a subtle art and, for most of us, requires continuous practice.

Try to watch the present moment. Can you catch hold of it? Can you find it, define it? Maybe we hear a short, sharp sound such as a bird cheeping in the garden outside. Was that cheep a moment? Then perhaps we hear the drawn-out whine of a passing moped. Was that a long moment, or a succession of short ones? If it was the latter, then where were the 'joins' between the moments? In that drone of the engine we don't seem to hear a succession of moments, but rather one continuous flow of sound.

Then, as we are paying really close and careful attention, we hear that the engine noise is not constant, but stutters, rumbles, and changes pitch as the driver slows and accelerates. Each different sound that we distinguish: is that a distinct, separate moment? Again, if that is so, how do those moments join together to form the continuous flow of experience? We never perceive any 'joins', so where does one moment end and another begin?

Has a new experience arisen in awareness because of the passing of time? Or has an experience of the passing of time arisen because of the moving on of awareness? To ask the same question in different words: has our attention latched onto something new because *time* has moved on, or are we experiencing the next moment of time because our *attention* has moved on? A moment: is it an instant of time, or an instant of attention? Or is it somehow both together? Is a 'moment' actually part of the process of paying attention itself?

No joins, but a flow of experience. Each experience arises and falls away again. It is not there, and then it is there, then not there again. It seems like the future pours over the razor-edge of the present, tumbling into the past. How 'thick' is that boundary; how long does it take for future to flow into past? It can seem like the arising and ceasing of the moment happens *immediately*; the moment comes and goes in an instant. However, if it really were immediate, how could we have experienced it? Surely the moment needs to endure for at least a while in order to be perceived?

Then again, if it endured for a certain while, how could the moment be only a single moment? Even a tiny length of time can be divided up into a beginning, a middle, and an end. So that cheep of the bird, for example: was it really one moment, or was it three moments? If it was actually three, where were the joins between them? As we noted before, we seem to experience a flow, not 'dots' of time following one after the other.

Each of us tends to maintain the notion that our life is comprised of a flow of moments in time: 'moments' that are 'in' something called 'time'. When we investigate this closely, we are left contemplating something much more mysterious. If a moment endures for a period of time, then it must be divisible into a start, a middle section, and an end. This means it can't actually be one moment. We can keep dividing it up until we have infinitely small instants that we couldn't actually experience. There wouldn't be enough time in which to experience them! But then again, a moment needs to have a beginning, middle, and end, because the start of one moment has to link to the end of the previous moment, in order for there to be a flow of time. We end up going round in circles: the moment can't be instantaneous and it can't be not-instantaneous.

To put it another way, a moment can't be either singular or plural; it can't be 'one', nor can it be 'many'. This is not just a limitation of concepts and language. By looking carefully we can see that experience doesn't actually happen 'in moments'. Experience isn't actually 'in time'. Time is an integral part of how we have experience of things. For there to be experience, the mind needs to 'hold' an object in awareness. This means it conjures up a sense of time (and space) to hold it 'in'.

An intrinsic part of the experience of anything is a time that it happened in. It is equally true that, for us to perceive a moment (or moments) of time, there needs to be some 'thing' that we experience. Perhaps you noticed this when meditating on the moment. We can only pinpoint a moment by looking for an experience of *something*, something that has popped into awareness *now*. Time, awareness, and objects of awareness are mutually dependent; the existence of any one of them depends on the others.

We might think 'it is always now', or 'it is only ever now', that 'life happens one moment at a time', and 'the present moment is the only moment', but these are only relatively true. Whilst thinking 'it is only ever now' may be helpful, it is, as Buddhist teacher Rob Burbea points out, more deeply true to say 'it is never now'. There isn't enough time for it to ever be now![91] The language of 'being in the now' may be a helpful call to awareness, important because that awareness is key to what we will become. It is how we respond to feelings of pleasure and pain right now that determines future experience. *That* is what is vital about the now. It is not that now is a more 'real' place to be; such thinking will only lead to grasping and attachment. As the Buddha said:

What went before – let go of that!
All that's to come – have none of it!
Don't hold on to what's in between,
And you'll wander fully at peace.[92]

Development, surrender, and emergence

Another reason why the language of 'now' is popular and current is the problem of wilfulness. Our practice of the Buddha's teaching can sometimes become too goal-orientated; we long for amazing meditation experiences, or gauge success by the presence or absence of special insights or altered states of consciousness. Perhaps this is also connected with our cultural conditioning; many of us come to the spiritual life from a highly individualistic and ambitious culture in which the ideal is always in the future, and the present is merely the means to that future. This individualism can make for insecurity; we have to prove ourselves, we have to stand out, and we also aspire to fit in. Many people seem to suffer from low self-esteem, and much consumer culture teaches us that self-worth comes from status, success, and possessions.

We can then import all these ideas and attitudes into our spiritual life. We may not rely so much on worldly success and possessions, but may come to measure ourselves by spiritual experiences and attainments, imagining that these will bring self-worth. We put ourselves under the same kinds of pressure to those operating in the mundane world. No wonder the language of 'staying in the now' should then become so appealing. 'Accepting ourselves' rather than striving for an ideal future, 'being' rather than progressing on a path, letting go rather than getting going: it all sounds much more attractive, helpful, and expressive of what we twenty-first-century human beings really need.

There is truth in all of this; wilfulness *is* an issue. Sometimes I have a ball of anxiety deep in my guts, and I try to relax and release it in meditation. I think I am trying to let go, but, very subtly, I am actually pushing the unpleasant experience away. It is understandable that I should want it to go away. The trouble is that I then take a stance of willing it, *pushing* it away, sometimes quite subtly, so that I am not aware of what I am doing. There is an underlying aversion to experience, which then perpetuates the tension. In these situations we need to rest *into* the anxiety, just be *with* the feeling of insecurity, to accept it rather than fight it. Wilfulness is a futile attempt to shortcut the process of transformation of heart and mind, either due to aversion (to emotional pain or discomfort) or due to craving (for some pleasant experience or sense of attainment).

This brings us to the great paradox of the spiritual life: how can the ego attain non-ego, what can the ego do in order for non-ego to arise? The answer is also paradoxical: we have to practise as best we can, and we need to let go and know we cannot *make* it happen. Enlightenment is not something that our ego can will into being. But we can orientate our hearts and minds in the right direction, and then be open and receptive, even entreating and inviting that 'enlightenment' to become a force in our lives.

A commonly used analogy is that of a lightning conductor. It is impossible to predict or control where lightning will strike. Yet it is possible to build a lightning conductor and point it towards the skies, which will make it more likely that lightning will strike right there. Our Dharma practice is like building such a conductor, pointing it in the right direction, and making ourselves ready and receptive to something from 'beyond'. We create the best kind of 'receptor' that we can. But we also have to let go of expectation; the 'lightning' of wisdom won't happen when we expect it, because expecting, hoping, or anticipating all entail a tightening of the ego.

In the Buddhist tradition, this paradox has been addressed in various ways. Different 'models' or metaphors have been employed in order to explain how the Dharma life unfolds. What is the best way of thinking about how we make progress, or how we allow Enlightenment to shine through into our lives? Our underlying model will condition how we approach practice, so this is not just an abstract question. According to a very helpful essay by Buddhist teacher Subhuti, there are three main 'myths' of how Enlightenment occurs. I am going to refer to these as 'development', 'surrender', and 'emergence'.[93]

A very prevalent metaphor for how the Dharma works is that of 'development'. Buddhism is a path from samsara to nirvana, from non-Enlightenment to Enlightenment, gradually transforming greed, hatred, and delusion into generosity, love, and wisdom. We strive to develop and evolve, we put energy and effort into changing habits and tendencies; we challenge ourselves now for the sake of freedom in a brighter future.

A second metaphor, perhaps less commonly to the fore, but nevertheless present in many places in the tradition, is that of 'emergence'. Enlightenment is seeing the true nature of reality. But that reality isn't anywhere else, it is right here and now, if only we could wake up to it! Our Buddha nature or Buddha potential is present all the time, just waiting to be discovered. Striving towards a distant goal merely reinforces the ego; it actually prevents the luminous nature of our mind from shining forth. We don't need to fixate on the future; all we need is here, right now. We can simply relax, let go, and trust that our true nature will emerge.

'Surrender' is another metaphor or myth, one found in its clearest and most uncompromising form in Pure Land Buddhism, but also featuring throughout the tradition. In order to stop suffering from craving and aversion, we need to give ourselves up to the Buddha, to Enlightenment. Again, any effort on our part is useless; we have so much craving and aversion to overcome. Better to surrender, to serve something greater and more enlightened, and to ask the Buddhas to help us.

These metaphors may seem contradictory, yet all three are found within traditional forms and articulations of Buddhism. And each has its advantages and disadvantages. For now, we are going to compare and contrast 'development' and 'emergence' (though we are not omitting 'surrender' because it doesn't have a role to play).

Thinking of our spiritual life in terms of development can be very helpful. It brings a sense of clarity and possibility; we are on a journey and what we need to do is just take the next step, and then the next one. This can give a sense of initiative; we feel we can *do* something. Doing, having a go, builds confidence; we grow in conviction that we can progress, that, if we practise, it will have an effect and help carry us along on our journey. However, taken in the wrong spirit, the idea of development could become wilful and forced, too fixated on goals and attainments. Our spiritual life then becomes too hard and narrow, lacking receptivity and a sense of wonder. If progress doesn't happen in the way we expected, we can become despondent and think we have failed. We can see the path in overly linear terms (ethics leads to meditation, which leads to wisdom) and, knowing our ethics and meditation aren't perfect, we think that someone like us could never experience real insight or wisdom. So we limit our idea of what is possible.

The path of development can look long and steep, its goal like a lofty mountain peak hidden in cloud at an impossible altitude and distance. The metaphor of emergence, by contrast, affirms our potential, and emphasizes that we are basically, innately, pure. This can be inspiring and encouraging. Emergence can encourage an attitude of receptivity and openness. But it can become too passive, so that our practice lacks edge and focus. I have definitely experienced this myself; at one stage in my life, too much emphasis on 'just sitting' (meditating without a specific focus of awareness, or any structure to the practice) meant that I did not engage effectively with the forces that were at work in my mind. 'Emergence' may bring with it a risk of subtly 'settling down': 'accepting ourselves' turns into no longer challenging ourselves to go beyond our ego clinging. With the development model there was a danger of an over-linear approach, whereas with the emergence model there might be an undervaluing of ethics as a necessary basis and preparation for insight. That might sound unlikely but, sadly, it isn't. There are well-known cases in the history of Buddhism where people have put themselves above ethical guidelines, committed seriously harmful acts, and then justified their behaviour in terms of Buddha nature.

There are also numerous stories in the Buddhist tradition[94] of practitioners who have striven for years, practising diligently and faithfully. Maybe they have lived an austere life, dwelling in a cave, eating little, a threadbare robe their only possession, and for years ardently meditating. Or perhaps they lived with hundreds of other monks or nuns in a monastery, devoting themselves completely to the communal life, and the daily routine of rituals, work, and study. After decades of practice they feel they are somewhat changed, they have become a better human being. And yet, fundamentally, they know that they are still functioning according to the dictates of self-clinging. That breakthrough into freedom has never happened. A spiritual crisis ensues; they have worked and worked, but all that striving has got them nowhere. What can they do? They couldn't possibly push themselves even harder. Thrown into doubt, they undergo a kind of spiritual breakdown: they give up, they surrender. And then, just then, a deeper and more decisive shift in the direction of wisdom and compassion occurs.

Such stories are surprisingly common, even 'typical', and this is instructive for us as we compare our metaphors of development, surrender, and emergence. For these stories contain all three: first development, then surrender, then, and only then, emergence. Clearly the latter couldn't have happened without the former. Those practitioners threw all their energy into development, gave themselves to it completely, so that they could then surrender completely. Only because they had fought that inner battle so tenaciously did they reach the point where their ego was willing to surrender. Then something totally new and different could emerge. They had to follow the path in order to arrive at the realization that the path didn't lead anywhere.

First we use 'development', then 'emergence'. Some current Buddhist discussion, however, underplays the development metaphor. Maybe some people have taken the metaphor in an unhelpful and wilful kind of way and got stuck with it, until they discovered the idea of emergence. What can happen is that we then kick against any idea of development. We need, however, to take care not to overgeneralize from our own experience when speaking to others about how practice works. We should be very careful not to dismiss either metaphor; we need a sensitive and intelligent combination of them, which is what you find in the best of Buddhist tradition. Some contemporary Dharma comes too heavily down on the side of emergence, sceptical of development. There is a bias that you can detect in the language used. But most of us will need to call on both models at different times in our Dharma lives. We need both 'development' and 'emergence'.

To link this to the 'lightning conductor' analogy used a few pages back, there is the work of erecting the conductor (development), and then there is the care and attention required to stay tuned, to listen carefully (emergence). In one's Buddhist life, it is probably helpful to think predominantly in terms of 'development' for a number of years. Gradually, however, our practice builds its own momentum, which can feel more akin to 'emergence'. That said, it is also important to balance them right from the start. In our meditation practice, for example, we can intersperse 'developmental' practices with 'just sitting'; we can look for a rhythm that will help break up any tendency to wilfulness and grasping. We do the practices with effort and engagement, and then we have times where we simply try to stay aware and receptive, without deliberately directing our minds, but just seeing what happens.

Perhaps it is best to have to hand as many metaphors as possible; they can then counterbalance and critique each other in helpful ways. If we did want to choose just *one* metaphor or image, however, maybe the best of the bunch would be that of 'growth'. This is represented in the classic Buddhist image of the lotus growing up through the mud, breaking the surface of the water, and blooming in all its glory. Every plant needs certain conditions in which to thrive and be healthy. It needs enough sunlight and water, enough shelter from the wind and certain nutrients in the soil. Human beings also need supportive conditions; without them it would be very hard for us to grow.

We can't rush the growth of a plant. Digging up a seed to see if it has germinated is worse than useless. We need to plant the seeds carefully, make the effort to water them, and to fertilize the young plants. But once we've done those things we just let the plant grow in its own time. Each type of plant grows in its own way. Some grow fast, some grow slowly. Some are naturally tall and straight, others more spreading and bushy. We, too, have to grow in our own way. We can't look at a big impressive tree over there and decide we are going to grow *exactly* like that. It is fine to be inspired by other people and their qualities, as long as we know that we need to grow according to our own nature.

When a plant grows, you don't always see it straightaway. Roots are developing, spreading, and growing stronger, but completely invisibly. We might feel that nothing is happening as a result of our meditation, but it might just be happening deep down where we can't see it. So we can think of our Dharma practice as like gardening, or propagating. This requires deliberate effort to help the plants 'develop'. But it also involves patiently letting the plants 'emerge' in their own time.

Imagining the future

Viktor Frankl was a psychiatrist who was imprisoned in several different Nazi concentration camps, including Auschwitz. He survived, and went on to write about life in those camps, describing how the men he was with struggled to survive, not just physically, but also emotionally and spiritually, in such horrifyingly cruel and degrading conditions. His extraordinary account, *Man's Search for Meaning*, has sold millions of copies all over the world.[95]

Frankl observed that it was a prisoner's relationship with the future that determined his well-being:

> The prisoner who had lost faith in the future – his future – was doomed. With his loss of belief in the future, he also lost his spiritual hold; he let himself decline and became subject to mental and physical decay.[96]

It was as if the present and the future no longer had any reality for that man, and he retreated into extreme apathy and lifelessness, or into retrospective thoughts.

Sometimes remembering happy events and recalling loved ones from the past was beneficial. Escaping into the past could help someone cope with the grimness of the present, but only provided they had not lost faith in the future. Frankl came to see that the few who survived were the ones who could find some kind of meaning or purpose, even in those appalling and inhuman conditions. Any attempt at helping a fellow prisoner

> had to aim at giving him an inner strength by pointing out to him a future goal to which he could look forward.[97]

Frankl himself used to imagine that one day in the future he would be giving lectures on the psychology of the concentration camp. It was having such a goal or aspiration that made life liveable.

'Being in the present', and only that, would have been utterly unbearable for Frankl and his fellow inmates. Their present experience was intensely bleak and painful, with no end in sight, except in death. They needed imagination to deal with their situation, to lift themselves above it and see a bigger perspective or meaning.

Internment in a concentration camp is surely one of the most extreme circumstances imaginable, but we all need goals and aspirations. 'Being in the present' doesn't mean not having a conception of the future and something to aim for. It means, however, that you build that future out of the bricks of the present; you imagine what could arise out of your actual life, and from your real thoughts and emotions. You live in imagination, but not in an escapist fantasy.

I have a friend who has suffered periodically from bouts of depression. He has used mindfulness meditation to learn to spot the harsh, self-critical, unforgiving thoughts that can send him spiralling downwards. 'Not judging' and 'acceptance' were helpful strategies, empowering him to work with depressive thoughts whenever they arose, to see that those thoughts were unhelpful and destructive, and that he didn't need to believe them. However, he was also left wondering: what was the point of not being depressed? If his life became free of depression, then what was that life *for*? 'Acceptance' isn't the goal of Buddhist practice, though it might be part of a helpful strategy for freeing us of negative emotion, and arriving into a space in which the true creativity of our mind and life can emerge.

We can't live without dreams, aspirations, something to aim for. However, we also need the courage to live out the dreams that are underlain by love, generosity, and wisdom, rather than the fantasies fuelled by craving and aversion. To do this, we need to learn the difference between reflective thinking and unreflective obsessing, between imagination and fantasy. 'Being in the present', in the sense of mindfulness – being able to watch thoughts and emotions, and to choose which ones to believe in and encourage – is a crucial part of this ability.

A charity known as the Karuna Trust, which operates mainly from the UK, works with some of the most oppressed and underprivileged people in India. One of the main ways in which the charity raises money is through door-knocking appeals, run by a small team of Buddhist volunteers who come together for a six-week period.

During the appeal each volunteer has a personal target, and their running 'score' is written up on a chart. This means each member of the team can see how everyone else is doing. Competitive, target-driven Buddhists: isn't this a contradiction in terms? The targets, however, are an essential component of the appeal. Karuna once tried an appeal without them and much less money was raised. There is, even for an experienced fundraiser, intense resistance to knocking on a stranger's door and asking for money. It takes particular courage, since there will be *immediate* feedback, an instant sense of 'success' or 'failure' that raises the stakes and that can cause anxiety. There is also fear of rejection, of being turned away empty-handed, or having a door slammed in your face. To overcome this resistance, the fundraisers need to be as motivated as possible. Without the targets, the temptation would be to take it easy, or to knock off early on a bad day. This would allow the resistance to grow stronger, eventually bringing them grinding to a halt.

The targets are there to help each person do their best. The volunteers also work as a team, helping and supporting each other to reach the collective team target. Those targets are an essential motivating force. At the same time, the fundraisers are not pressurizing or haranguing people on the doorsteps; it is their wholeheartedness and genuineness that will be most persuasive.

One of their mottoes is: 'no expectations, only possibilities'. Having an aim gives us direction, energy, and purpose, as long as we don't fixate on it and expect our efforts to bring about exactly what we had hoped. Sometimes we don't aim for anything because of fear of failure. We don't want to suffer the imagined pain or humiliation of failure, so we protect ourselves by being 'cool' and pretending we're not bothered. At the other extreme we can become fixated on goals and overly driven. The middle way is to form goals and aspirations, but to hold them intelligently, without too much expectation, staying open and willing to learn from whatever happens.

Dwelling in possibility

In this chapter we have ranged around quite a number of topics, though all related to this notion of the 'present moment'. 'Being in the now' can help us drop clinging to the past, or craving for the future. But we can also reflect thoughtfully on the past, or plan helpfully for the future. The difference is in the type of emotion that is taking us into past or future, and it requires mindfulness, presence, to know and stay aware of which type is driving us. It is that presence that makes the present vital.

There is, therefore, a freedom to be found in 'being in the moment', dropping the fantasy past and future, and letting go of the clinging and craving that makes them seem so fixed and urgent. But there is an even more profound freedom to be discovered by looking deeply into the nature of that moment, and seeing that it isn't real, in the sense of being self-existing, separate from our attention and awareness.

If we can do this, we see just how radically our experience is produced by mind. The nature of our awareness and attention determines what unfolds in experience, including the sense of time that things unfold in. To see through this container of time is

153

to be 'uncontained' – to dwell in an expansive freedom. We 'dwell in possibility' in the subtlest, most profound sense, fully seeing and knowing the ever present creative nature of mind.

We see the mind-made nature of time. And yet, precisely *because* time is an intrinsic part of how our minds work, we do also need to work *with* time. In this chapter we have also explored the relationship between the present and the future. Having goals, aspirations, or targets corresponds to what we called the model of development. Staying open and flexible, free of expectations, corresponds to the model of emergence. The paradox is that we need both simultaneously: no expectations, but always possibilities.

We do need to imagine or envisage the future. Yet we also hold it lightly, always remembering that it is just imaginary: imaginary, but necessary, even crucial. We can't take our stand on a fixed future or outcome: life will never provide that kind of certainty. Conversely, if we are full of doubt and fear, shrinking from the future, and sticking only to what is safe and familiar, then our creativity and dynamism won't flower either. The future is a mystery growing from the soil of the present. We can plant the right seeds and tend the seedlings, and we can do so with faith and confidence that something good will come of it. We can work *with* the process of growth and unfoldment, though we can never grasp or control it.

Part III

In the fullness of time

Patience

It's a weekday morning and I'm sitting rock still, eyes closed, meditating. Inside my mind there's a puppy, off the leash.

He darts hither and thither, sniffing, barking, wagging his tail. He runs ahead and then sits waiting for me. His black coat is glossy, shining; out hangs the big pink tongue. His eyes are bright white and watching.

As soon as I am near, he runs away again.

He comes back clenching a stick, looking hopefully at me. No, I'm not going to throw the stick. Put it down. Let it go. His jaws clamp around the stick tighter than ever. He gives me that doggy-sorry look: why won't you play with me?

Can I meditate with this puppy in my mind?

He runs in a circle three times, chasing his tail. He catches a sudden scent and dashes off in pursuit. Eager as ever, he comes trotting back, looking pleased with himself.

Now he bounces round my legs, nearly tripping me up. With a shock I open my eyes: I'll be late for work! Yet, according to the clock, barely two minutes have passed.

All that running around: what time did it happen in?

I close my eyes again, and – tail wagging – he comes bounding up to me, that puppy in my mind.

11 o'clock

Buddha time

So how would it be if we could give up craving and aversion? How would it be if we completely let go of self-clinging? In particular, what would happen to our sense of time? In other words, how would a Buddha experience time?

Is it possible to answer this question? Can we really imagine the experience of an Enlightened being? And if it were possible to connect with such a sense in our imagination, could we really give expression to it in words? Maybe we can have some inkling of what it might be like, albeit very tentatively. We can think back to times of deep contentment, or total absorption and engagement, or beauty and inspiration. Perhaps in those situations time has unfolded more seamlessly and effortlessly, there have been hints, or more than hints, of timelessness. There have been some occasions when I have been immersed in nature where I have caught a glimpse of that possibility. Now imagine being *fully* like that, and imagine *always* living from that 'dimension', or at least being continuously in touch with it and able to access it.

Experiences of seeing through time can manifest in different ways for different people. One friend of mine described a period in which his experience of time and space could radically shift. He would be walking down the hill to the train station where he lived, in a state of relaxed awareness. Perhaps he was in a phase

159

of doing more meditation than usual, or his meditation had been deeper. And then time and space would just change:

> In one sense, I'm walking down the hill from my house to the station. But, in another sense, my experience is not one of moving. Everything is flowing past me, 'I' am still. Everything becomes clear and bright, more colourful and alive. The more I relax into it, the stiller I become and the more there is just a sense of 'now-ness'. The last twist of the tale is that the more I allow myself to go with this, the less 'objective' ordinary time on the watch it seems to take to get to the station. A pure 'objective time' makes no sense at all when in this experience.

The Buddha, time, and eternity

Traditional accounts of the Buddha's Enlightenment describe a series of three visionary realizations that took place at different stages through the night, whilst he sat meditating under the bodhi tree. Here, we are concerned with the first two visions.[98]

In the first, the Buddha saw that he had been born and reborn countless times. He saw how he had lived a certain kind of life at one time, and this had meant him being reborn in particular circumstances later on. As far back as he looked, he observed this process rolling inexorably on. In the second vision he realized that the same was true for all living beings everywhere. He watched infinite numbers of beings being reborn in different states of existence – into heaven or hell realms, into human or animal worlds, into states of joy or woe. Again, it was an endless cycle, with no beginning and no end in time or space.[99]

Later on in the development of Buddhism, these visions were represented pictorially in the image of the wheel of life, with its great turning wheel, the six realms of existence, and the twelve links in the chain of becoming. I used to struggle with these traditional descriptions. How could the Buddha really, literally, see *endless* lives? Wouldn't that also take an endless amount of time to witness and comprehend? Apparently he saw it all in the course of a single night. How could that be possible?

I was taking the story too literally. Maybe this traditional account is attempting to point us to an experience beyond our usual frameworks. The vision of endless past lives is a vision of vast time; the vision of countless other beings being born in numerous different worlds is a vision of vast space. Or, to put it another way, the vision of his previous lives emerged out of a profound *depth* of awareness, really seeing into the depths of the mind and the traces that have been left there by previous thoughts and actions. Then that awareness expanded outwards and took in all life, all existence; the vision of countless beings born and reborn arose out of an extraordinary *breadth* of awareness.[100]

In other words, that vision of past lives is symbolic of deep and complete integration. The inner psychic forces that, before he became the Buddha, drove the young prince Gautama into an always receding future had been brought into awareness and transformed. Those forces would drive him no more. He had stopped running; the wheel had stopped turning. There was nothing lurking in the shadows that could catch him. He had nothing to regret from the past and nothing to strive for in the future. He saw a whole life going back. It was as if he had taken it in all at once. And then he saw further back, lifetime after lifetime. Again, it is seen all 'at once'. Everything is there at that moment, all time is poured into that unified totality. He 'holds infinity in the palm of his hand and eternity in an hour'.[101] All of his struggles, hopes, failures, disappointments, and triumphs had led to this moment, which spiralled out again into the mystery of the future.[102] That eternity wasn't some kind of unending time, more a seeing deeply into the nature of things. That vision of 'eternity in an hour' was a vision of interconnectedness, of this moment, each moment, as a nexus that links all the past and all the future. For the Buddha this was a lived and felt experience, a *knowing*. Of course, it is not that he really saw eternity *in an hour*, for that would still be within time. He saw eternity in no time at all. Time had unravelled into timelessness.

The morning star appears in the sky. There is a golden glow above the eastern horizon. Dawn is approaching. The Buddha opens his eyes. He is Enlightened, though he also still has his human body with its sense faculties and mind. He still sees the tree towering above his head, hears the sound of the river, and feels the cool night air against his skin. The world (in space and time) still appears to him. Yet he now knows it is not completely real in the sense of existing just like that, independently and separately from his perception of it. But nor is it completely unreal, either.

Perhaps he hears birds starting to sing and he looks about him. He takes it in and feels a ripple of joy shimmer through his being. Something is different. He is not tied down into that fixed point of self around which time turns. He is not backed up into that separate point of self around which space fills. It all still appears, time passes, space opens out, but he is not tied up inside it, or alienated from it. He knows it all for what it is. He sees it as a play of appearance: rainbow-like, diaphanous, luminous.

The fixed point of self around which there can be a 'now', and therefore a past and a future, has been seen for what it is – a provisional reference point. Past, present, and future are therefore also provisional; they are how life appears from a particular slant of time. Not overidentifying with this fixed point means his perspective expands; every moment is eternity. The flow of time may be part of his experience, but it is not absolutely real or ultimate, and this means that the Buddha can be lighter, freer, and more equanimous.

There is the Buddha, embodying Enlightenment in this world, his mind and senses still functioning, and therefore the world of space and time still manifesting for him. He sees the world is full of living beings running around in samsara. So the Buddha also functioned in that world; he worked with the world of time. There was no conflict or resistance. If you read about the Buddha in the Pali canon, you don't get the impression of an individual out of touch with lived reality, zoned out in mystical states. Instead, you encounter someone eminently practical, engaged with the work of creating a living spiritual community, and very able to meet and communicate with a wide range of people. He seems to have lived quite a regular, disciplined lifestyle. There was a time in the day for the almsround, for walking and sitting meditation, for Dharma discussion. There were times of the year for wandering and teaching tours, times of the year for the community to gather together and stay in one place. Sometimes there would have been practical reasons for this: the rainy season retreats, for example, were organized to prevent monks from travelling through rural areas at the time of year when wandering on the young and tender crops would damage them. Perhaps also the routine and disciplined lifestyle were helpful to the monks, and so the Buddha lived that way to encourage them and to exemplify a life of Dharma practice. It was a full life, and one with a steady, predictable rhythm, though there were also times when the Buddha slipped away into the forest for a while to be alone, to refresh and enjoy the full depths of his inspiration.

No time tension

One senses the Buddha didn't waste his time. Nor did he allow other people to waste it. The early texts recount a number of instances where, meeting someone and feeling that they would not be receptive, or were just trying to pick an argument, or were just engaging in vague speculation, the Buddha brought the conversation to a close and moved on. However, he gave his time freely and fully to all those who wanted genuine communication.

The Buddha knew that time was one of the forms of his (and our) being. How you are is how your time will be. He knew that time was not separate from him, not like a container into which he could try and fit as much as possible. Time was not a 'thing' he could have, or a 'medium' that he was in. There would, therefore, never be any grasping at time, never any time tension. He would not waste the slightest quantum of energy worrying about or fighting time. Of course there might be objective limitations and constraints on his time. But they would never have pressured him into craving and aversion, and this means they never tensed up into a tight sense of self. There was always a plenitude of well-being within him, a sense of abundance that included the temporal.

There is a story about the Buddha meditating in a forest clearing when a king, in a horse-drawn chariot, with his retinue, travels by. This is not actually a true story, but is derived from, and draws the same conclusion as, a debate between the Buddha and some ascetic practitioners that is recorded in the Pali canon.[103] The king notices the Buddha, calm and quiet, sitting under a tree, seemingly doing nothing at all. The sight touches the king in some way, even challenges him – though perhaps he is not yet aware of why. He orders his men to stop, climbs down from the chariot and approaches the Buddha. Despite the commotion of men and horses, the noise of hooves and turning wheels, the Buddha's eyes had remained serenely closed, but now he opens them and with a smile greets the king.

The king wants to know who he is, what he is doing there, and why he looks so happy. The Buddha tries to explain but the king is sceptical. He cannot believe that a man with nothing except a robe and bowl could really be happy sitting under a tree doing nothing.

Surely he, a king, with soldiers, advisors, musicians, courtiers, and minions, must be happier?

'I am not so sure', says the Buddha, and he asks the king if he could sit with him under the tree, quiet and content, for half an hour? The king replies that of course he could. 'Could you sit there totally still for an hour?' responds the Buddha. Slightly more hesitantly, the king replies that he could. What about half a day? Now the king is chewing his lower lip and looking doubtfully at the ground. 'Maybe I could manage it', he finally answers. What about a whole day? But this is too much for the king. 'Of course not,' he bursts out, 'there is no time for that, there are too many orders to give, messages to receive, parades to attend, banquets to organize.'

'I could sit here, perfectly still and content, not worrying in the slightest about even a single thing,' said the Buddha, 'and not just for a whole day, but for a whole week, or even longer. Therefore I think I am the more fortunate and happy one.'

In the ordinary human state we always seem to be busy, driven on by the next thing, oppressed by time. However fast we run, we can always hear time running just behind us, breathing down our neck, just about to catch us up, just about to place its hand on our shoulder. The race against time is one we can never win. We have to change the rules, play a different game. In the king, craving was still running, still running him, still dictating his life and behaviour, despite the fact that he was a king of great wealth and power, with command over many men and women.

When there is no longer any craving, we have all the time in the world. There is a plenitude of time. The Buddha knew how to get a lot done, but without being 'busy'. He could give the gift of time from a sense of abundance. There are many stories of the Buddha giving his time. He always gave it freely. Even on the Buddha's deathbed, a man came who wanted to meet him. He was turned away by those attending the Buddha and told it was too late. But the Buddha overheard what was being said and called the man over. His name was Subhaddha and he became the last personal disciple of the Buddha.[104]

Giving time to others

Reading the traditional accounts, you sense that the Buddha really met people, fully gave them his attention, and took them in completely. Often he had an uncanny ability to connect with others quickly and understand what was going on for them. This was probably a result, at least in part, of that quality of attention. I know a couple of people who met the current, fourteenth, Dalai Lama. In both cases, they noticed the way he fully attended to each person. Even if he was going down a queue of people shaking their hands, for the few seconds he was with you, he was wholly and solely with you. Even if he only had a few moments to give, he totally gave them. He wasn't already halfway moving on to the next person. On both of my friends this made a deep impression. We really value the gift of time and attention. As the French philosopher Simone Weil wrote to a friend, 'Attention is the rarest and purest form of generosity.'[105]

In the 1970s, social psychologists ran a research project that became known as 'The Good Samaritan' experiment.[106] A group of theology students were asked to prepare a presentation as part of their studies. Some were to give a presentation on empathy, some on a more neutral, value-free topic. They were then sent, one by one, to another building to give their talk. On the way, they had to walk through an alleyway, along which, clearly visible, was a man on the ground, obviously sick, in distress, and needing help. Unbeknown to the students, the man was an actor, hired to play this role by the researchers. Would there be any difference in response between the students about to give a talk on empathy, and those about to speak on a neutral topic? Perhaps surprisingly, there was no difference. About the same number stopped to help as carried on past, regardless of the topic they were speaking on.

But there was another variable that did make a significant difference. As they were sent over to the other building, some of the students were told: 'Oh, you're late. They were expecting you a few minutes ago. You'd better get moving.' A second group were told: 'The assistant is ready for you, so please go right over.' And the third group were told: 'It'll be a few minutes before they're ready for you, but you might as well head on over.' In other words, there were 'high urgency', 'low urgency', and 'no urgency' groups.

Only 10 per cent of the high-urgency group stopped to help the apparently sick man. Ninety per cent of them carried on past, some even stepping over the man whilst on their way to give a talk about empathy! However, a much higher 63 per cent of the no-urgency group did stop to help. If we are in a hurry, head down, wanting to get somewhere fast, then it is obviously harder to take anyone else into our awareness. All the students would have *seen* the sick man, but a higher proportion of those in a hurry seemed unable to *empathize* in that moment. And what if our life involves being *habitually* in a mad rush? What effect will that have? If our time tightens, our heart hardens. Habitual time urgency (as opposed to a real emergency) narrows down our awareness, disconnecting us from other people. We end up snapping at our children as we try to prepare them for school on time, only half listening to our friend telling us their troubles, or forgetting that the person on the other side of the post-office counter is another human being. Time-sense and empathy are interconnected.

To live egotistically, to be overidentified and overconcerned with a fixed point of self, is to live trapped and tensed up in time. But it is not that there is an illusory realm of time and then a real dimension of eternity. We are not trying to *escape* from time into eternity. They are the same reality viewed from different perspectives. An Enlightened being realizes them both simultaneously. No longer self-preoccupied, he or she neither grasps nor resists a time conceived as separate from them. They realize the true nature of time, and therefore they realize eternity. They now identify with a totality that transcends the individual. But that vaster perspective also gives each moment extraordinary depth, richness, and plenitude. They can give themselves at every moment without resistance or effort. They can give their time out of love and compassion. For us too, if we can let go of our self-preoccupation and concern ourselves more with the needs of others and what needs doing in the world, then our time will become 'free'.

Living in time that is both bounded and open

There are many stories in the Buddhist tradition of practitioners striving for years, searching for Enlightenment. Suddenly (and sometimes unexpectedly, when they had almost given up) they break through into realization. They laugh as they see that what they were looking for was right there all along. What they discover seems so obvious and natural; how foolish not to have seen it before now! Such stories show us that Enlightenment is not just the result of practising hard enough for a long enough time. Eternity isn't waiting at the end of a long line of time; it is a different experience altogether. However long we go on, we will never get any nearer to it. And now, in this very moment, we are right next to it. We are as near to it as we have ever been.

If Enlightenment is 'out of time', this doesn't mean that, once achieved, it lasts forever, stretching on into an endless future. If it is 'out of time', then it has *always* been achieved. And yet, to accomplish it we need to practise. As Sangharakshita puts it,

> Contrary to our usual metaphorical mode of description, Enlightenment is not reached by following a path. But this doesn't mean that the path should not be followed.[107]

168

There is a sense in which time is unreal, just an 'appearance'. But it really does appear; we can't deny or ignore that appearance! We need to live in the world of time. We could say there is 'ultimate truth' (an Enlightened being's perspective), and then there is 'relative truth' (the perspective we need to take in order to be able to 'approach' Enlightenment). So what might be a helpful 'relative truth' about time? One answer is well expressed in the saying: 'Live today as though it is your last day. But it will last for 1,000 years.'

We need a sense of the preciousness and fleetingness of time in order to live life well, to use our time wisely and prioritize what is truly important, valuable, and meaningful. This is living from the perspective of 'one day'. But it doesn't mean rushing at life, trying to cram our time full to bursting point, always urgently racing to some imaginary finishing line.

To live a fully human life, one in which we can actually *appreciate* what is important, valuable, and meaningful, we need to feel we have a plenitude of time. We need patience, to allow things to take the time they take. This is living from the perspective of '1,000 years'. Paradoxically, we need to do both: to simultaneously live 'one day' in '1,000 years' and '1,000 years' in 'one day'.

There are, obviously, objective constraints and pressures on our time. We do indeed only have limited time. Reflecting on a teaching such as the 'four reminders' can help align us with the perspective of 'one day'. This puts us in touch with what really matters in our life, or what is most important and urgent right now. It helps us prioritize.

Actually, we *need* boundaries and limits; coming up against them, learning how to respond to them, can draw out our creativity and ingenuity. It is like writing a poem in a traditional form, such as a sonnet or haiku. In English, a sonnet must have fourteen lines, ten syllables per line, and a particular rhyme structure and rhythm. In Japanese, a haiku has only three lines and seventeen syllables, and there must be five of those syllables in the first, seven in the second, and five in the last line. Why set rules in this way? Why limit the numbers of lines and syllables? Why define where the rhymes and stresses have got to be? Isn't that just going to constrain the creativity of the poet, shackle their imagination? No – in practice, it can help to release creativity. Working within the form of a sonnet forces the poet to look for novel solutions. They need to work with words like never before, weave words into new spells to work new magic. They conjure up lines and phrases that otherwise would have remained undiscovered. The 'external' limitations unleash an inner creativity and freedom.

The form of a haiku imposes such severe restraints, and yet thousands upon thousands of haikus have been written. What might initially seem like an impediment allows for something distinctive to happen: just one or two seemingly simple images, and then the short last line that gives them added meaning or poignancy:

Even in Kyoto –
hearing the cuckoo's cry –
I long for Kyoto.[108]

The poet is tied down, and yet this allows his or her imagination to fly free. It is *because* they are tethered in the one way that something else is set loose. The form isn't a fetter, the form is freedom.

Time is perhaps the predominant 'form' of our human life. There can be stark limits on our time. But if we can work with those limits skilfully then, again, creativity is drawn forth and set free. We are forced to be resourceful, to use our resources carefully, to be effective and efficient, and to get on with it.

Being creative: time and aliveness

I was once part of the organizing team of an outdoor event attended by a few hundred people. It was the last day of the event, and we needed to dismantle the big tents and pack away the canvases. However, rain was forecast for the middle of the day. For the organizers this was bad news. So we asked as many people on the event as possible to help us quickly dismantle the tents. Very soon we were joined by scores of people in rows, pulling on ropes, lowering ridge poles, folding sheets of canvas, the team members with the loudest voices bawling out instructions. The atmosphere round the site became energized, focused, full of laughter, and the tents were all packed away before the rain started. A time-pressured situation transformed into a wonderful opportunity for cooperation and camaraderie. It brought people together and raised the collective spirit onto another level.

Our lives are bounded, rounded with a sleep. And yet we also need to feel we have all the time in the world. If we aspire to live a creative life (creative in the broadest sense, not only in the artistic sense), then we need to be alive to what lives below the ordinary scheme of things, rather than busily skimming over the surface. It is harder to be creative if we feel hemmed in by time. Also, if we are grasping too hard for the 'result' or 'end point', this tightens up our mind, makes it less wieldy and malleable, and this stifles its potential. Creativity requires a certain relaxation and letting go, trusting that the natural abundance of the heart and mind will reveal itself.

Although time may be short, we can't be in too much of a hurry. If we hurry (in the grasping sense, not in the sense of doing things quickly and efficiently), then time will tighten up and this makes it seem even shorter. We need the perspective of '1,000 years'. We need to feel there is ample time. We need to remember that the importance of any endeavour is not just what lies at the end point, but also how we get there. That *how* will determine the *what*. Or, as Friedrich Nietzsche puts it:

> Not every end is a goal. The end of a melody is not its goal; but nonetheless if the melody had not reached its end it would not have reached its goal either.[109]

The composer Rossini apparently said that the best time to compose an overture to an opera was the night before the first performance. There was, he said, nothing like it for concentrating the mind. In 1599, Shakespeare wrote not one but four great plays: *Henry V*, *Julius Caesar*, *As You Like It*, and *Hamlet*. He could turn out several plays per year, at the same time as acting, directing, and running a theatre business. There is also the well-known story behind the creation of one of Dostoevsky's novels.[110] His brother had died, leaving the family in a dire financial position. Because he was desperate, Dostoevsky sold the publication rights to all his works to a businessman called Stellovsky. In the deal was a clause stipulating that Dostoevsky had to produce a completely new novel by November 1866, or forfeit all royalty payments for nine years. In that same year, however, he was already trying to complete his novel *Crime and Punishment*, and he carried on with that well into the summer. He didn't actually start work on the new novel that was contractually required until October. He gave himself just four weeks to write a novel, or else face financial ruin. The novel, appropriately enough, was called *The Gambler*. On 29 October, with two days to spare, he completed the novel and submitted it to Stellovsky. Despite the extremely pressurized circumstances, Dostoevsky had managed to write a psychologically astute and darkly comic depiction of addiction to gambling.

Do these examples contradict the idea that creativity needs time? Rossini seemed to relish leaving the creation to the last minute. Perhaps he had, actually, already written the overture in his head, and what he was resisting and leaving to the last minute was the more irksome task of committing the music to paper. Or perhaps a creative genius is able to tune into that creativity at any time, or in no time. They can just stop whatever else they are doing and the plenitude of '1,000 years' is there, waiting for them. Rossini, for example, was confident he could access '1,000 years' within the limits of 'one day'.

As Buddhist teacher Ratnaguna points out:

> [E]ntering into the 'timeless realm' doesn't necessarily require a lot of time. 'Timeless' doesn't mean 'lots of time'. We need to feel that we have all the time in the world, even though we may not – because, of course, we never do.[111]

Even if, by the clock, we have only 10 minutes to spare, we can still enter into a timeless realm. We do this by letting go of utilitarian goals and targets, giving up treating time as a commodity or a fixed container.

We need to be able to live from the perspective of '1,000 years', even when time is limited. This is far from easy; maybe it is a lifetime's practice. Perhaps it is especially difficult for us twenty-first-century human beings living in the 'age of anxiety'. But it can be done, even in difficult circumstances, as the following example illustrates.

It is a story told to me by my friend Elaine, whose grandmother, whom she was very close to, was old and sick. One day Elaine received a phone call to say her grandmother was dying. There was not much time left, she had to reach her grandmother as quickly as possible. Would she arrive in time? Time, of course, raced by; it became tight, urgent, and contracted. She sprinted down the busy high street, agitatedly weaving through the crowds of shoppers and schoolchildren. A large flock of pigeons scattered into the air as she shot by, and suddenly something shifted. Amid the sound of flapping wings she heard a voice say, 'She's here.'

Elaine stopped running and felt immensely peaceful. She realized that she was *already* connected to her grandmother. In her heart and mind right now, she could be aware of her and close to her. She could walk along – at a good pace, but not a frantic one – sending loving-kindness to her all the while. Running against time seemed futile: that human connection was right there and now, not in an imaginary future. She didn't want to arrive at the hospital in a state of anxious panic, unable to be present. The most important thing was to be present *now*. Awareness and loving-kindness totally changed and expanded Elaine's perspective; they enabled time and space to be transcended. She carefully reflected on the loving words she wanted to say to her grandmother whether she was still alive or not (and thankfully she was).

We need our time to be both bounded and open. If we live only from 'one day', then our perspective changes into a 'near enemy'. We can become overwilful; we habitually operate in a mode that is speedy, driven, and urgent. Our time becomes tight and, consequently, our minds and hearts less open and sensitive; it becomes harder to empathize with others. Perhaps this is the 'clock time' default setting of much of our contemporary culture. If we live only from '1,000 years', then that lopsidedness is also liable to distort into a near enemy: a laziness and apathy in which our time drifts aimlessly, loose and unstructured; we waste time, procrastinating, and our life flits by. Maybe later we look back, ruing 'the time torn off unused' (to quote Philip Larkin).[112]

We will probably have a temperamental inclination one way or the other. Some of us are so driven that we need to learn to waste time. Some of us need to learn to set goals and to plan and use time efficiently. Perhaps, to start with, we can think of 'balancing' the perspectives of 'one day' and '1,000 years'. We try to ensure there is time for both of them in our lives, both work time and play time. We notice our own personal bias and we learn how to create more balance. If we do this, then, gradually, 'one day' and '1,000 years' will start 'blending', and we can consciously encourage and practise this. If we need to meet a deadline, for example, we practise retaining a sense of spaciousness. There can be calm during time-defined activity.

Eventually 'one day' and '1,000 years' become so perfectly blended that there is no longer a polarization between them.[113] They are perspectives that are always there for us. We know they will be there, so we can just relax, trusting they can be called on. We can glide smoothly between activity and receptivity, between focus and openness. To borrow an image from the Zen teacher Dōgen, we swim on the surface of the ocean (the world of clock time, of activity and necessity), whilst our feet walk along the bottom of the ocean (the perspective of depth, spaciousness, and plenitude).[114] We can flow into the mode of 'one day' or '1,000 years' as appropriate, according to the situation and what others need from us.

12 o'clock

Play time

Even though right now humanity overall enjoys more material wealth than in any previous era, many of us commonly declare that we don't have enough time. Even though we can benefit from all sorts of time-saving machines and devices, and more leisure time than our forebears a century ago, we can feel time-pressured like never before. Psychological suffering caused by stress is reported to be at record levels, and much stress is time-related. Living too much in a time-urgent mode is exhausting, and cuts us off from our deeper emotions and potential. It can also hinder a more heartfelt connection with others.

Our relationship with time profoundly affects the quality of our lives. In the last few years this topic has been much discussed in the mainstream media. The psychology and neuroscience of time perception have also recently become major areas of research.[115] The growing world of secular mindfulness has emphasized the importance of being in the present. Numerous books have been written about the benefits of living life more slowly, and articles published about work–life balance.[116]

Busyness might be described as a modern religion; it is part of a story, a belief system, very prevalent in our culture, about how happiness is to be found in the future. Deep down, however, we may intuit that our habitual way of doing time is a crazy fantasy, the dis-ease of the twenty-first-century world.

This book has explored our relationship with time with reference to the teachings and perspectives of Buddhism. We have been exploring time from a number of different angles. Chapter 1 pointed out that our actual experience of time speeds up and slows down, dependent on our state of mind, particularly on the quality of our attention, and also on mental and emotional states of craving or aversion. Longing for something to change and pushing away from current experience slow and stretch our experience of time. Clinging to the current state of things and being averse to change speed and contract that experience. A particular mindset is also a particular experience of time; the two are interrelated.

Chapters 2 and 3 gave an account of the world of clock time and how we may be culturally conditioned into certain ideas and practices in respect of time. These have their practical uses, but can we forget that they are just a social convention and make them into something more fixed and real? Can clock time become a 'fetter', a 'rite and ritual as an end in itself'? Can we end up fitting our life to the hour, rather than the hour being a tool that may help us to live our life?

Chapters 4 and 5 delved into the way in which human beings are storytelling creatures. Inside the privacy of our heads, but also in conversation with others, we constantly narrate our lives. We have stories about how we got to where we are now; we call that the 'past'. We also have stories about where we are going and how we are getting there; we call that the 'future'. In our experience right now, past and future don't exist, except as stories inside our individual and collective awareness. These stories can be more or less helpful or unhelpful, opening up or shutting down human possibility and creativity. There are ways to shine the light of awareness into the way we tell stories. In particular, we explored 'healing time' and the need for forgiveness towards what has happened in our past.

Play time

Even if there is much about our experience of time that is created in the mind, surely there is also an objectively existing world that is changing according to certain causes and processes? Surely, then, if there is an objective world, there is also an objective time? Isn't my human life of a given span, regardless of what I may think about it? Chapter 6 investigated the way we experience change, tending to think that it happened 'in' time, as if there could be a time separate from change. It is not that things change because time passes, but rather that we experience time passing because things change. Time is our idea, framework, or perceptual and conceptual apparatus for experiencing change. Subsequent chapters explored Buddhist teachings and practices that address our attitudes to change.

This theme continued in chapter 9, considering how time is 'tensed' into past, present, and future. But 'now' depends on an observer; it is subjective, perspectival, and past and future only exist relative to that 'now' that is the present. Again, we discovered how time-sense is one of the 'forms' built into how the human mind constructs experience, how it perceives and makes sense of the world. In chapter 10 was an invitation to examine our actual experience of time, asking: is a moment an instant of time, or an instant of attention? If we look carefully, we can see the mutual dependency of time and awareness. We see how strange and mysterious the unfolding of our experience is.

So where (or when!) does this leave us? Is time real or unreal? Is there an objective time, or is it purely subjective? In a way, these categories are too crude and clumsy. There is no big grandfather clock ticking away somewhere in outer space, measuring an absolute, objective time. Time is a sense that arises in human awareness, or that is part of how the human mind generates experience. Yet that experience arises in dependence on the world around us: it emerges out of a relationship with conditions that are changing independently of our perceptions and volitions. Time is how self-aware humans conceive of 'things' that are 'passing', coming and going past the supposedly fixed point of 'me'.

And what does this then mean for how we relate to, and deal with, time in our lives? Perhaps the main theme running through the book is the interdependence of self-sense, time-sense, and the mental and emotional states of craving and aversion. To grasp or repel creates a tighter sense of self, and of time. To be more mindful and equanimous brings a more open and flowing sense of self and time into being. This is a choice we are making at every moment of our lives. Whether we are conscious of it or not, we are always choosing and creating the quality of the time that we live 'in'. Buddhist practice entails examining and opening out the assumptions about, and experience of, that self at the centre of experience. It involves practising the giving up, or letting go, of craving and aversion, seeing how this leads to a much more liberated, expansive aliveness. It will also create a more 'timeless' experience, one unconstrained by craving-created time. That leaves us with time for others; we are able to give the precious gift of attention and empathy.

So how to answer that question of whether time is real or unreal? On the one hand, time isn't absolutely, objectively real. If we can unpack our assumptions about it, and see clearly the mutual conditioning of self, time, and craving, this can help us give up craving more radically and thoroughly, leading to a deeper, fuller freedom. On the other hand, clearly we can't treat time as totally subjective, and therefore completely unreal. Time is innately part of human experience, and we have to take notice of it, and work with it. In fact, if we are skilfully aware and respectful of time, this can also help prevent us clinging to life in ways that constrain and limit us. Time is telling us about change, reminding us that we can't hold on. Noticing the quality, the texture, of our time can teach us so much about the deep, subtle habits of craving and aversion that box our lives in. Examining our relationship with time can be powerfully transformative.

Ten time experiments

This final chapter centres on ten practical suggestions for 'playing' with time. Once we become more aware of the attitudes and behaviours that distort our sense of time, we can respond differently. Our experience of time, which means our experience of our life and everything in it, can become more healthy, happy, and human.

I have used the word 'play' to encourage an approach that is explorative, experimental, and enjoyable: playful rather than utilitarian. That relationship with time won't necessarily transmute overnight, but it can gradually shift, and eventually it can change more deeply and decisively. The process of 'playing' with time offers a chance to discover and learn many other things about ourselves: what winds us up, what makes us tick, how the whirring cogs of the mind are constantly fabricating a world of experience. What the mind creates is not just the *content* of that experience, but its very *form*, including the time that it seems to be 'in'.

1. Notice time distortions
The first practice is to bring awareness to our experience of time. Where and when does our subjective sense of time alter or distort? When do we feel time-poor, or time-urgent? When does time seem to be racing, and when crawling? What is going on right then? Can we look under the surface of our experience, dig down beneath the speedy thinking, and unearth the emotions and volitions that are causing the distortion? Do we sense a feeling of 'driven-ness' or 'avoiding-ness'?

The feel of our time can tell us something valuable about what is happening inside us. Time can be like a mind mirror; time can be a teacher. The feel of that time is a real *experience*, but that is all it is – an experience created by our mindset and behaviours towards what is happening. And a different experience will come about if we can change the mindset and behaviours.

Try especially to watch what happens in situations of stress and urgency, where our stance can easily tense, and so tighten up time. These are times to pause, step back, bring our awareness into the physical body, breathe deep into the belly, and feel our feet on the ground. What do we need to do to regain perspective, and to start to loosen that screwed-up knot of time?

2. Take time out of time

By this I mean not living always ensconced in *clock* time, not doing every activity by the clock, not measuring and assessing every moment of every day according to the clock's criterion. Of course we can't avoid clock time, and it can be extremely helpful and useful. This practice is about us being able to use clock time, but without it taking us over. One way to help avoid its overdominance is to take breaks from it. Clock time doesn't have to be the one and only mode in which we function.

What does this mean as a practical proposition? It might mean very small things. For example, I have a friend who commutes daily into London. From his local station there are trains every few minutes, but he always used to aim to catch the 7.27am, not the 7.24 or the 7.33. Often this meant leaving only just enough time, and then rushing out of the house at the last minute. Then my friend realized he didn't need to be so fixated on the clock. The morning routine didn't need to be quite so exact, muesli munched to the minute. As long as he was roughly aware of the hour, he could stroll to the station and catch the next train that came along, and still arrive punctually.

Zoe, another friend of mine, recently undertook a three-month retreat in a remote mountainous area of Spain. The team running the retreat encouraged the participants to forget about clock time; they consciously made this part of the ethos of how they tried to live and practise together. The daily programme was posted up only a day at a time, rather than a week in advance, to encourage people to be with what was happening that day, rather than anticipating and jumping ahead. There were bells to mark the start of mealtimes and activities, so they didn't need to be constantly checking their watches. It was suggested that, if they kept a journal, they didn't write the date, but allowed themselves to forget what day of the month it was. The tendency could have been to count the days and weeks, to calculate how long they had been on retreat, or how long was still to go. By leaning backwards or forwards into past or future, rather than simply being present, they would partially absent themselves, become somewhat removed emotionally and mentally. Instead, they were encouraged to give themselves as fully as they could to each day, to being completely there, to being there and only there, whatever was happening. This might sound strange, even potentially manipulative, but Zoe didn't experience it like that. She was amongst supportive friends whom she trusted, and she found it liberating and revelatory. She found herself being more fully and continuously present than at any previous time in her life.

We might not all have the opportunity to participate in such a retreat, to step out of clock time so completely and for so long. Still, we can all arrange or allow for interludes that are not timed. We can create spaces in our day that are less structured by the clock, where we just let things take their time, where we can attune to our own inner rhythm. We create gaps in our day where we don't operate in that mechanical, clockwork, time-urgent mode. By opening up those gaps, we help break up the underlying driven-ness and it starts having less hold over us. More occasionally, at weekends, on holiday, or on retreat, we can create the possibility of doing this for longer.

3. Zen and the art of waiting

One aspect of playing with time is learning the waiting game, how to deal with waiting and boredom. When there is an empty space of time where it is not possible to move forward towards our goal, what do we do? In these types of situations we can often try to push against time; we become impatient, then we feel bored, then we seek distraction. Sometimes situations of waiting also involve being anxious (a bus is late when we need to arrive for an interview on time), or being tired (a bus is late after a long and busy day), so these are, in a small and everyday kind of way, challenging situations; we become wound up into craving or aversion, creating that tangle of self and tightening the knots of time.

Yet even when there is no time pressure we can still find waiting difficult. We may feel restless; we feel we *ought* to be doing something. We find ourselves jumping up and doing a few small chores. Recently I was sitting in a friend's house, waiting for him to arrive. He had a chess set laid out on its board on the coffee table in front of me. I suddenly found myself tidying up the pieces, adjusting them so they were lined up more neatly.

It can be surprisingly tricky to stop and do nothing. The energy we have been using up till then has its own momentum. That energy wants an outlet and so we feel restless, or the energy feels stuck and we feel bored and sleepy. This then feels uncomfortable, and we're tempted to make ourselves busy again, or to distract ourselves, to avoid the discomfort.

In these periods of boredom we are writing off the present; we think that what matters is in the future, and now is just a tedium we have to twiddle our thumbs through. If our attitude is one of wanting the present to pass, to become past as quickly as possible, then it will feel empty and hollow, like a lifeless vacuum. The antidote is to come consciously into the present, to attend to what's happening within us and around us, right now. We put ourselves actively in the present and wait there, receptive to what that moment can reveal to us. If we can wait in this positive sense, then we will find everything we need is right there, waiting for us too.

Zoe, the same friend who told me the story of her three-month retreat, also told me of an experience she had waiting for a train at Ealing Broadway station in London. The battery on her mobile phone had just gone flat, and so she thought she had nothing to do. Perhaps there was even a tinge of dread and panic at the thought of all that empty time! However, Zoe found herself opening out and becoming more aware of her surroundings. Gradually that awareness became more fully sensitive and alive. Down the railway line, maintenance work was under way, producing a constant metallic clanging and hammering. At first the noise was jarring, but then it became more musical, and then it seemed as if the bustling crowds of commuters were filing back and forth to that rhythm, dancing round each other. It became absorbing and beautiful. Platform 2 of Ealing Broadway station transformed into a realm of timelessness.

Another situation in which we can try to push through time is when we are doing chores that we find dull and irksome. On the one hand, human beings need enjoyment, stimulation, stretch, and not to be doing tasks that are mind-numbingly dull and repetitive for too much of the time. On the other hand, there will always be a certain amount of work to be done that is routine. Again, instead of seeing these occasions as dead time, and merely an obstacle to the future, can we turn them into a practice of living actively and alertly in the present, doing the tasks with more care and attention?

4. Effective time management

Perhaps we might feel sceptical of the whole 'time management' industry, suspecting that it has no concern with efficiency and effectiveness in a fully human sense. Nevertheless, managing and using our time well are basic skills that will make a big difference to our general well-being. To achieve any goal, we need to know both where we are aiming and the immediate next steps to take us in the right direction. In other words, we need to know the long-term aspiration and the short-term priorities.

One aspect of this skill of using time effectively is to distinguish 'urgent' from 'important'. This is the basis of one of the most famous time-management models, devised by Stephen Covey.[117] The most valuable lesson I learnt from this model was to make time for activities that are 'important but not urgent'. These activities tend to be squeezed out when we are feeling busy, and many of us *always* feel busy. Important but not urgent is time for thinking and reflecting, studying, stepping back and considering, looking into new ideas and possibilities, or sharing open-ended conversations. (In a way, it is like stepping into the space of '1,000 years' rather than always functioning on the basis of 'one day'.)

If we wait until we feel we have enough time to do the 'important but not urgent', then most likely it will never happen. We need to *make* time for the 'important but not urgent'; we need to write it in our diary and prevent anything else from invading that space.

Another commonsense technique is to compile lists. If we are carrying around in our head all the things we need to remember to do, they take up more mental space, and we are more likely to forget some of them, or be unable to prioritize them as necessary. A list in my head always feels longer and more onerous; once I've written it down, it is never as long as I had thought it would be. Writing it, externalizing it, helps to see it objectively. Suddenly it feels more achievable and I feel less anxious. The list may be comprised of two or three sublists: things I need to do today, tasks that need to be completed this week, and then longer-term reminders and goals. Once I've ticked off one or two items on the 'today' list I feel a sense of achievement. And if there is more on the 'today' list than I can actually do in one day, then I can't do it! This isn't the end of the world. It is time to think: can I delegate, or ask for help? Or what can I put off till tomorrow, or what do I simply cut out? Overbusyness is the delusion that I *have* to do everything or the sky will cave in.

5. Spare time

We need time to do nothing. Lots of nothing. Relishing, glorifying, in doing nothing. Just to sit with a cup of tea and gaze out of the window, and not to do anything, say anything, prove anything, be anything, find anything, solve anything, or any other type of anything. Spare time is time to take a complete break from having to be 'me', to put aside the masks and uniforms, the badges and name tags, the job descriptions and to-do lists.

As Jon Kabat-Zinn says, 'If you fill up all your time, you won't have any.'[118] So are there ways we can simplify our life, or reduce input? Can we create empty spaces in our life; can we 'spare time'? This practice is slightly different from, but overlapping with, the second practice that focused on unstructured time, time that isn't clock-watched. We might do useful activities without measuring and judging them by the clock. The point I am emphasizing now, however, is to have time in which we don't need to do anything 'useful' at all. We can just watch the wind ruffling the leaves on the trees outside, or jot down thoughts in our journal, or listen to music. It is time for the non-utilitarian, the 'useless' things that are what all the 'useful' parts of life are actually *for*. Sometimes the so-called 'useful' things take over and become ends in themselves; we lose sight of the real point of it all.

Perhaps, when we first sit and do nothing, we feel anxiety rising from the pit of our stomach, an urge to do something, to justify our life, to reassure ourselves that we are worthy of existence! As I described under the suggestion about 'waiting', it can be quite a challenging practice to stay with these feelings, but not to obey them, to relax and wait until new life arises from somewhere even deeper than the pit of the stomach. The temptation is to jump up and start doing something 'useful', or to distract ourselves in some way. We can become speed addicts. Stopping and doing nothing can feel worse before it feels better. But, as Nietzsche wrote,

> He who completely entrenches himself against boredom also entrenches himself against himself: he will never get to drink the strongest refreshing draught from his own innermost fountain.[119]

We need to shift gear gradually. And we need to be prepared to wait and to maybe go through a phase of boredom. If we can do this, something different will eventually bubble up into awareness. Imagine gazing into a deep rock pool. If you wait still and silent, and if you do it for long enough, gleaming silver fish emerge shyly out of the seaweed, bright-coloured crabs clamber out from under pebbles, sea anemones unfurl their coral-red tentacles and sway them to and fro. But it requires that wait; if we move about too quickly and impatiently, then we never see anything.

Sometimes we can't believe that, if only we wait, something good will emerge. Therefore we don't wait, and therefore it doesn't emerge, and that reinforces our lack of belief in our own depth and potential. My friend Tom says it takes him 7 minutes of doing nothing before his mind 'clicks' into a different mode; something shifts and his awareness becomes less utilitarian and more aesthetic. Our nervous system is wired up to get us to act on our impulses; the feelings it produces in the body – twitchiness in the limbs, a surge of energy in the belly, a feeling of lack in the heart – are the brain's mechanisms for getting us moving. But these feelings and cravings come and go surprisingly quickly. We just have to be prepared to wait, to do nothing, for maybe 7 minutes, until our brain switches gear.

6. Meditating on time

Throughout this book are various suggested meditations on time, looking directly at our experience of time, and seeing how we might have played a part in its creation. Here is one more meditation on time. (For more detailed instructions, see 'Reflection-meditation 6' in the appendix, pp.207–8.) It is the practice of trying to drop the past and the future, and, instead, just be present with experience as it arises and passes away. If your mind drifts during meditation, where does it tend to go – backwards into the past, or forwards into the future?

That time travel is happening in our heads, so can we get 'underneath' it? Shifting our awareness to and focusing it on the body, especially the heart and the belly, can help. Can we feel the basic 'driven-ness' or 'avoiding-ness' that is causing us to drift? Can we then try to 'unhook' the story about the past or future from the urge, and just feel that raw, basic energy? Like the practice of 'doing nothing' described above, this requires a willingness to stay with feelings of anxiety or insecurity, to actually relax *into* them. If we can do this, then the energy can start to change. It is like an alchemical process in which *we* are the base material that will be transformed into gold, but only if we can rest in that fiery crucible and be willing to melt, to release and let go. We are trying to see through our narrow, limiting investment in past or future, and to stay with the present. (Though of course there is also a place for more *conscious* reflection on the past or future.)

You might even drop simple phrases into your meditation. If you see yourself replaying an earlier event in your mind, you can tell yourself: 'Just drop the past.' If your mind races ahead to the future, you can say: 'Just drop the future.' Once you find yourself more in the present, you might even try saying: 'Now drop the present.' Try it and see what happens!

The film *Into Great Silence* took the viewer into a Carthusian monastery high in the French Alps.[120] The monks lived an extremely simple and austere life of prayer and contemplation, mostly in solitude, interspersed with routine daily tasks. Life went on, pretty much the same, day after day, year after year. For those monks there was, in effect, nothing to look forward to. Tomorrow, and then the day after, would be just the same as today. To some of us, the idea of not having anything to look forward to might sound quite negative, even horrifying. But what those monks were practising was a deep and thoroughgoing 'living in the present', not living for an imaginary future that then created a sense of *waiting*, and of their lives being always provisional, on hold, until they got to where they really wanted to be. The routine of the monastery was designed to help the monks totally surrender to life – to live without thought for their future, or even their present.

Not all of us could live this way. Perhaps, though, it is good that some people live like this, as a kind of reminder and teaching to the rest of us. We may not be ready to practise 'living in the present' quite so radically as those monks, but we can still practise dropping the past and future, trying to drop desire, so we enter more fully into a deeper life.

7. Stories that create time

Chapter 4, 'Story time', considered how the past becomes the future through the lens of the present, through how we view and interpret the past in the present. We have habits of perception, or, putting it another way, we have certain stories we tend to tell ourselves again and again. This radically conditions the person we will become. So can we be more conscious of our stories? Can we notice what we have invested in them? Can we start to leave aside the unhelpful ones, the small stories that limit us, or that are demeaning to other people? Can we also notice our stories about the future, where craving and aversion, combined with the inherent unknown-ness of that future, create anxiety and more stories, expectations, and assumptions that try to fill the knowledge vacuum? Can we practise not knowing, or, at least, give the future the benefit of the doubt and have more positive assumptions and expectations?

To live a more human, creative, free life, we need to develop 'integration'. Often this is described as a *spatial* wholeness: bringing into harmony our depths and heights, our head and heart, or the different sides of our personality, or aspects of our psyche. But we can also think in terms of a *temporal* wholeness, a sense of continuity and congruity from our past to our future, having a sense of awareness and purpose around the fact that who we are today, how we think and act, will determine who we are next week, or next year.

One last point under this heading: it can also be helpful to notice the stories we tell about time itself. We may have a narrative that is habitual, even part of our identity. I may constantly be telling myself, for example, that I have too much to do, and not enough time, and how am I possibly going to fit in all in? Such stories can become unthinking and automatic. What is the effect of telling such a story, and how true is it really? What would be a more helpful narrative about our time?

8. Techno time

It can be important to notice what the use of technology (by which I mainly mean digital, electronic technology) does to the quality of our time, its texture, viscosity, the ease with which it flows. Does using a digital device swallow up huge gobbets of time, leaving us wondering where the day disappeared to? Can it fragment our attention, so desiccating the subjective feel of our time? Which technological devices really do save time – and what do they save it *for*?

I certainly benefited from being able to write this book using a word processor, and researching via the internet. However, used unreflectively, some technology may be doing very particular things to how our mind works, keeping us in 'fast thinking' mode, and making that more predominant. Let us use technology with awareness and discernment. Whilst using it, we can make a special effort to stay mindful of our bodies and the sensory world. We can also enjoy time offline so that we can see if this leads to a different experience of ourselves, including time for 'slow thinking' mode.

9. Take a trip into vast time!

Sometimes it is good to take ourselves out of the particular little bit of 'space-time' that we are identified with, to be expanded beyond our usual preoccupations into a much vaster perspective. We don't need to travel anywhere to do this; we don't need a TARDIS or a time-travel contraption. We already have our imagination. Art and culture can help us glimpse beyond our everyday identification with the here and now; they can expand our consciousness beyond the 'me' that we tend to think is at the centre of the universe. Good films and novels involve us intimately in the lives of others, perhaps with those living in very different cultures or times of history to our own. The best science fiction takes us far out into space and way into the future. Learning about the scientific study of the stars and the vast universe, or studying geology and the formation of landscapes over vast time, or understanding natural history and the gradual evolution of ecosystems, can open out and expand our awareness in space and time. Immersing ourselves in myth and legend can also help us touch into something timeless and universal, giving us that strange sense of transcendence.

I have a friend who says he cured himself of anxiety through expanding out his sense of time and space. If he found himself brooding anxiously about something, he would imagine that thing within the context of a larger and larger time frame. How all-important would it be in a month, or a year, or 10 years, or 100, 1,000, or 1 million years? And then, similarly, he viewed it in a more and more spacious context: how important would his preoccupations be relative to what was happening in the city he lived in, then the whole country, the continent, the world, even the solar system and the whole universe? How urgent and all-encompassing did it seem then?

Problems and issues that, from our subjective frame of reference, seem like enormous boulders weighing down on our shoulders are seen to be just tiny insignificant specks in the story of the universe. Of course this doesn't mean ignoring difficulties, or trying to pretend they don't exist. This was my friend's tactic for dealing first and foremost with his rumination and worry; this then opened more mental and emotional time and space, and that enabled a more creative response to emerge. He said that, practised again and again, over months and years, this really helped him transform a long-standing tendency to anxiety.

10. Overcoming craving requires a vision

A central concern of this book has been how craving and aversion confine us inside a twisted, contracted box of time. If we want to break free from the pain of this narrowness, then we need to go beyond craving and aversion. But we can't simply stop them, just like that. Our energy, our volition and emotion, needs somewhere to go. We don't *stop* craving, we *sublimate* it; we transfer it somewhere more truly human, meaningful, noble, and altruistic. Human beings need a vision to aspire to, a cause or community to serve, friends and loved ones to care for, or wisdom or beauty for which to search. We need something more than us, into which we can pour our desire, energy, and creativity.

One of the Buddhist words for mindfulness is *sati*, which is etymologically connected to the word for memory or recollection. On the one hand,

> The faster we go, the more we forget, and the more we forget, the less we know who we are or where we are going.[121]

193

Free Time!

When we are speedy, when racing against time has become our default setting, this contracts our time and narrows our vision. On the other hand, when we are aware and mindful, allowing things to take the time they take, then we stay more recollected and present, and in touch with our purpose. That quality of engagement means our life flows and the oppression of time can drain away into the background. We can just give our time. And that makes our time full and rich, deep and brimming.

Appendix

Guided reflection-meditations

The following reflections and meditations have already been briefly outlined in the main text, but here you will find more full and detailed guidelines should you want to practise them for yourself.

Reflection-meditation 1: the four reminders

The four reminders are discussed in chapter 8, 'Reflection time', as the first of three suggested practices for contemplating impermanence. You could use these reflections at the start of your meditation – if you have a daily meditation practice – or at another time, while sitting quietly or going for a walk, for example. You first need a space free of distraction, some time being quiet and getting settled, and then you can start the reflection.

You could focus on one reminder for a week or so, and then move on to another. Or you could rotate them on a daily basis, doing a different one each day. Or you could do all four at once. You could read the relevant reflection slowly to yourself, line by line, a few times. Or you might know another piece of writing, a poem, or a song, that addresses the same themes. Just let the main message sink into your heart. There is no need to try to force any response; keep it simple and trust your intuition.

The idea is that, through sitting quietly and contemplating the four themes, they gradually drop down more deeply into your being. At first, your reflections may seem a bit abstract and artificial, but, with practice, they gradually become more emotionally real, and become part of you.

1. Impermanence and death

Everyone who has ever lived has also died.
Countless numbers of people have been born and passed
    away.
This will happen to me too.
One day I will have to face death.
I can never know when this will be.
It could be tomorrow, or next week, or next year.
Already my body is ageing,
I can see already how my body grows old.
All my friends and family, too, will pass away.
In a hundred years from now we will all be gone.
Life is fleeting, so I should remember this.
It is good to reflect on what will matter most at death.
It is good to live a life free of regrets,
Good to compose quarrels,
Good to use my time wisely,
And so resolve to make the most of my life.

2. Life is a precious opportunity

I'm alive and aware.
How extraordinary this is!
Today I will see so many forms and colours, hear so many
    sounds.
I can think and feel and use my imagination.
How amazing to be alive.
I have food, shelter, money, and all the basic necessities of life.
Many people in the world are not so fortunate.
I have family, friends, people who care for me.
We can communicate and talk – what a wonderful thing!
There is so much natural beauty in the world.
There is also art, music, culture, and education.
There are spiritual teachings that inspire.
There is so much of value in the world.
Do I make the most of these treasures?
Do I appreciate the precious opportunity of life?

3. Suffering

I can't entirely avoid suffering.
There will be times of illness and discomfort.
There will be times when life doesn't give me what I want.
Sometimes people, even trusted friends, will disappoint me.
All this is part of life.
It happens to me, and it happens to everyone.
So how should I respond to suffering in my life?
Life is constant change.
I will never get everything in my life to stay just how I want!
I should resolve to remember this truth.
All around me I see so much suffering.
On TV there are wars, famines, or disasters.
On the streets I see people suffering stress, old age, or lack of
    meaning.
In nature animals are hunting, or being hunted, always
    struggling for survival.
Sometimes I can act with kindness and relieve suffering.
Let me resolve to try to do this when I can.
At other times, I cannot take away all the suffering I see.
But at least I can remember and not forget.
And resolve to live the best life I can.

4. Actions have consequences

I am the product of so many complex conditions.
I was born into a particular country and time in history.
I had certain parents and family and upbringing.
All these things will deeply influence who I am.
But my own actions also condition my future.
What I think with my mind,
what I say with my voice,
what I do with my body:
All these change the person I become.
All these impact on the world around me.

Let me recall some of the good I have done.
There are times when I have offered help and friendship.
There are times when I've spoken true and kind words.
There are many occasions when, even in small ways,
I have made a difference to those around me.
I am responsible for my life and actions.
Let me resolve to act from the good.
Let me try to avoid harming myself and others.
Let me try to be a force for good in the world.

Reflection-meditation 2: yesterday, today, tomorrow

This is the second reflection on impermanence recommended in chapter 8, 'Reflection time'. An insight deepens into wisdom by being *made use of* repeatedly. Our understanding of the truth of a Buddhist teaching matures when we see it in experience again and again.

A good grounding in loving-kindness is necessary for these practices. If you find reflecting on impermanence lowers your mood, then pull back and try to address what is going on, perhaps by doing the *mettā bhāvanā* practice. If your mood lowers repeatedly or dramatically, then perhaps it is not the right time for you to be doing these particular practices, or at least not without the guidance of someone experienced.

1. Sitting quietly, spend some time 'grounding and arriving', feeling physical sensations in the body, and following the breathing in and out.

2. After, say, 5 or 10 minutes, turn your attention to what happened yesterday. Just allow memories of events, experiences, conversations, emotions, thoughts, and 'mental states' to come and go. As you do this, notice that all those experiences are gone now. They have disappeared into the past. Look at that flow of memories through the lens of impermanence, gently reminding yourself that all that seemed so real and immediate yesterday has faded away.

3. Then turn your mind to what you are experiencing now, and all that will happen today. Contemplate that experiences will arise and fade away in exactly the same way. When you look back tomorrow, how much will you remember of the minutiae of experiences today?

4. If you find it hard to keep your attention focused on these reflections, then it is fine and good to alternate periods of body awareness or breathing meditation with periods of looking at the impermanence of yesterday, today, and tomorrow.

Reflection-meditation 3: noticing change at every moment

This is the third and final contemplation on impermanence from chapter 8, 'Reflection time'. Developing wisdom requires examining our experience very carefully and closely, in subtle detail. We are endeavouring to see the habitual views and interpretations that are in play moment by moment. We are trying to notice, for example, tiny moments of attachment or fixating onto things – the tiny moments that, repeated over time, add up into the story of our lives. We try to catch them, and then try to give them up, or let them go, and then notice what happens, what it feels like to be free of them.

In order for this to be effective, some clarity and stability in meditation will be necessary. These don't need to be perfect, but you need enough of them to be able to stay with the reflection and be attuned to what is happening. Sometimes the reflection itself can help you develop that clarity and stability; at other times you need to switch to a *samatha* practice (such as the mindfulness of breathing).

1. Sitting quietly, spend time 'grounding and arriving', feeling physical sensations in the body, following the breathing in and out. You might also pay attention to sounds and sensations around you.

2. After a few minutes, also give your awareness to feelings of pleasure, or discomfort, or just feelings of neutrality. These feelings might be physical, emotional, or mental, or some combination of the three.

3. Now turn your attention to thoughts and images in the mind. Try and feel the 'quality' of that mental activity: are thoughts fast or slow, clear and definite, or vague and bitty? Or has the thinking mind quietened for now? Is there a prevailing emotional tone, or a mixture of emotions? Then also look at the 'content' of any activity in the mind: what are the thoughts, stories, images about? Is the mind tending to go into the past or the future, or go down certain 'tracks'?

4. The aim is to gradually establish a broad awareness of our experience. From here we begin looking through the lens of impermanence, seeing how experiences come and go in the mind: sounds and sensations, thoughts and images, feelings, volitions. Can you tune into that flow of experience?

5. Some experiences may come and go very quickly, whilst others may seem to last for longer. As you observe, however, you may notice even these subtly changing. An ache in the body, for example, varies in intensity and its precise location. The constant hum of the heating system goes in and out of awareness; the experience changes according to how we pay attention to it.

6. If experiences come and go, beyond my control or volition, can they really be 'mine' in any ultimate sense? If experiences come and go, beyond my control or volition, can they really be 'me'? Reflect in this way, with a spirit of lightness and letting go.

7. Come back to body awareness or awareness of the breathing as often as you need to, as a way of maintaining stability and grounding yourself.

Reflection-meditation 4: sense of self

This reflection relates to chapter 9, looking at the nature of 'self'. If you would like to try this reflection, then have a pen and paper to hand. You will need about 20 minutes, and somewhere quiet and undisturbed to sit, so that you can first of all physically settle and relax, and feel relatively spacious.

1. After a few minutes, bring to mind a recent situation in which you got irritated or defensive in some way. Try to think of a real-life example and to recall the experience as fully as you can. What was your sense of self at that time? What did it feel like to be 'you'? How did it feel physically, in the body? How did it feel emotionally, in the heart? How did it feel mentally – what was the tone and type of thinking that occurred in that situation?

2. After a while, allow this scenario to fade away, like clouds dissolving into blue sky. Then call to mind another recent situation, but one in which you were kind, generous, friendly, or helpful in some way, large or small. Try to dwell in the experience again. What did it feel like to be 'you' right then? What was your sense of self in that situation? What happened in the body, the heart, and the mind?

3. Once you have contemplated this long enough, allow it also to dissolve away into the blue sky. Lastly, try to remember a time in your life when you were at your very best, perhaps a situation in which you were deeply content, or inspired, or creative, or maybe an activity in which you were totally absorbed or engaged. One more time, ask yourself what your sense of self, of 'me', was like at that juncture. What did it feel like in the body, the heart, and the mind? Do you notice any difference between this and the second scenario, or is it like a stronger version of the same thing, or is there no difference? Once again, allow the thoughts and images to fade from the mind.

You can now open your eyes and take some time to write down what you noticed about the difference in your 'sense of self' in each of those three scenarios.

Reflection-meditation 5: finding a moment

This meditation gets us looking at our experience of time, and also takes an 'analytical' or 'deconstructive' approach to our ideas about 'the moment'. It relates to the discussion of the 'present moment' in chapter 10.

Like reflection-meditation 3, it requires that we establish a broad base of awareness, and enough stability and continuity in that awareness. We try to 'step back' in order to watch our own mind at work, to see experiences as they arise and fall in our awareness, but without either getting drawn into them and distracted, or pushing them away and avoiding them. This is quite a subtle art and, for most of us, requires continuous practice.

When you are ready, watch your experience carefully and closely. For example, notice sounds, or thoughts, or body sensations as they come and go. Try and watch the 'present moment'. As you do this, drop in some of the following reflections and questions. It is probably best to do just one at a time (e.g. number 3) and to repeat it, rather than trying to go through all five at once. Treat them like koans; you may not be able to answer them straightaway, and that is fine. They are intended to question our assumptions about our experience, and provoke us into looking at what is really going on.

I find these reflections work best by alternating thinking with returning to observing actual experience. It is fine to think and puzzle for a while, but don't let it get too abstract; come back periodically to what is happening in experience.

1. Watching the present moment, can you see where it comes from? Can you see where it goes? Watching the present moment, how long does it last? How long is 'now'? Can you catch when the moment starts and ends? If it is instantaneous, then how can you experience it? How could there be enough time to experience it? But if it is not instantaneous, how can it be only one moment?

2. *Watching what is happening in your experience, try to notice one moment at a time. Can you get hold of one moment? A thought or a short sound: is that one moment? That moment: is it an instant of time, or an instant of attention? Or is it somehow both together? Is a 'moment' actually part of the process of paying attention itself?*

3. *Do some experiences seem to be more of a continuous flow, rather than individual moments? Are longer sounds, for example, or a conversation in your head, not singular moments, but more of a continuous flow? Is that in some way related to how you are paying attention to that experience? Surely that flow of time must be divisible into smaller moments? The moment: is it defined by time, or defined by your attention?*

4. *Watching the present moment, how did it join onto the preceding moment? How does it join onto the next one? When or where are the joins between different moments? Do you experience the joins? If there is a flow of experience, how does it all join up?*

5. *If you find a single moment of experience, then surely that moment must have had a beginning, a middle, and an end? In other words, was it not made up of three shorter moments? And wouldn't those three moments also be divisible? Wouldn't you end up with instantaneous bits of time? Anything with a beginning, middle, and end must be divisible into smaller moments. But if a moment had no beginning or end, how could it come after the preceding moment, and lead to the next one? It would need a 'beginning' that lines up with the 'end' of the last moment. And it would need an 'end' that connects up with the 'beginning' of the next one. It needs to be divisible into beginning, middle, and end. To be one moment it needs to be divisible. And yet a divisible moment can't be just one moment, because, by definition, it can be divided into smaller moments. So how can a moment be possible?*

Reflection-meditation 6: unhooking past and future, expanding the present

This final reflection-meditation is about noticing when our mind jumps back into the past or forwards into the future, and, instead, trying to cultivate a sense of plenitude in the present. What follows is described as a meditation practice, but of course we are trying to learn skills that we can apply off the meditation cushion too. When we are feeling our time becoming tight and pressured, we can deliberately counter that by encouraging and imagining a sense of our time being open and expanded.

1. Once you have given yourself time to arrive and settle, follow the breathing in and out of the body, enjoying the sensations and flow of the breath. In this meditation, use the breathing as an 'anchor' for your focus and awareness.

2. If and when you notice your mind wandering, where does it tend to go – backwards into the past, or forwards into the future?

3. You might drop simple phrases into your meditation. If you see yourself replaying an earlier event in your mind, you can tell yourself: 'Just drop the past.' If your mind worries ahead into the future, you can say: 'Just drop the future.' Then come back to watching the breathing.

4. Sometimes that pull into past or push into future is more strong and insistent. If you notice it keeps happening, can you investigate it more deeply? Shifting and focusing our awareness to the body, especially the heart and the belly, can help. Can you feel the basic 'driven-ness' or 'avoiding-ness' that is taking your mind backwards or forwards? Can you try to 'unhook' the story about the past or future from the urge, and just feel that raw, basic energy? Can you breathe into that, soften it, and let it go?

5. Come back to the breathing, feeling all the richness of body sensations as the air comes and goes. Look for a sense of enjoyment and well-being. Can you savour the present moment? Can you see how rich and full it is? You might even try expanding your sense of the present.

Free Time!

Looking for a sense of 'spaciousness' can help. As well as noticing the feel of the breath, can we also dwell in the pauses between in-breath and out-breath, and then between out-breath and in-breath? What do those little gaps feel like? Can we notice the silences between sounds, the spaces around body sensations, even the pauses between the ticking of the mind, and the thoughts and images that it generates? Imagine that the next 10 minutes will last an hour! In fact, imagine that they are infinite! Quietly tell yourself that this moment is enough, and relax into its richness.

Notes and references

1   John Spurling, *The Ten Thousand Things*, Duckworth Overlook, London 2014, quote taken from front matter.

2   *The Sūtra of Golden Light*, trans. R.E. Emmerick, Pali Text Society, Oxford 1996, p.13.

3   For more on 'flow', see Mihaly Csikszentmihalyi, *Flow: The Classic Work on How to Achieve Happiness*, Rider, London 2002.

4   Robert Macfarlane, *Mountains of the Mind: A History of a Fascination*, Granta, London 2008, p.204.

5   Billy Bragg, 'New England', from the album *Life's a Riot with Spy vs Spy*. He adapted the lines from another song by Simon and Garfunkel.

6   Frédéric Gros, *A Philosophy of Walking*, trans. John Howe, Verso, London 2014, p.83.

7   Samuel Beckett, *Waiting for Godot*, Faber and Faber, London 1971, p.48.

8   Vidyamala Burch, *Living Well with Pain and Illness*, Piatkus Books, London 2008.

9   Vidyamala, *Living Well with Pain and Illness*, pp.27–8.

10 I have reimagined and retold this story from an original anecdote related in Natalie Goldberg, *Long Quiet Highway: Waking Up in America*, Bantam Books, New York 1994, pp.158–9.

11 You might ask what is wrong with wanting something pleasurable, or with desiring something good and helpful. Likewise, what could be wrong with wanting to avoid pain and trouble? We will be exploring the nature of craving and aversion further as we progress through the book. For now, however, maybe we can see that there is a difference between, on the one hand, having a wish or aspiration and, on the other hand, being attached to an outcome, staking our happiness on it. Craving and aversion have that quality of narrow fixation. They are inflexible and uncreative approaches to seeking happiness and satisfaction, as we think we can only be happy if we can have (craving) or avoid (aversion) that one particular thing, person, or situation.

12 Karma is how our volitions, whether manifesting as actions, speech or thoughts, have a conditioning effect on our personality and mind, and therefore help determine our future experience. For more on how this works, see chapter 8, 'Reflection time'.

13 Louis MacNeice,'The sunlight on the garden', in *Collected Poems*, ed. E.R. Dodds, Faber and Faber, London 1979, p.84.

14 Sangharakshita, *Living Wisely: Further Advice from Nagarjuna's Precious Garland*, Windhorse Publications, Cambridge 2013, p.105.

15 'The washing never gets done', in Jaan Kaplinski, *Selected Poems*, Bloodaxe Books, Tarset 2011, p.75.

16 Carl Honoré, *In Praise of Slow: How a Worldwide Movement Is Challenging the Cult of Speed*, Orion Books, London 2005, p.25.

17 Jay Griffiths, *Pip Pip: A Sideways Look at Time*, Flamingo, London 1999, p.5.

18 'Selections from the Arran Isles', in John Millington Synge, *Plays, Poems, and Prose*, Dent and Sons, London 1982, p.256.

19 E.P. Thompson, 'Time, work-discipline, and industrial capitalism', *Past and Present* 38 (1967), pp.56–97.

20 Thompson, 'Time, work-discipline, and industrial capitalism', p.61.

21 Thompson, 'Time, work-discipline, and industrial capitalism', p.89.

22 Thompson, 'Time, work-discipline, and industrial capitalism', p.86.

23 See, for example, Paul Glennie and Nigel Thrift, *Shaping the Day: A History of Time-Keeping in England and Wales 1300–1800*, Oxford University Press, Oxford 2011.

24 Paul Davies, *About Time: Einstein's Unfinished Revolution*, Penguin, London 1995, p.16.

25 Davies, *About Time*, p.30.

26 To understand more of the scientific exploration of time, I would recommend Carlo Rovelli, *The Order of Time*, Allen Lane, London 2018.

27 Yuval Noah Harari, *Sapiens: A Brief History of Humankind*, Vintage, London 2014, ch.2.

28 Quoted in Paul Kingsnorth, *Confessions of a Recovering Environmentalist*, Faber and Faber, London 2017, p.1.

29 Henry David Thoreau, *Walden: or, Life in the Woods*, Dover Publications, New York 1995, p.58.

30 Sangharakshita, *Buddha Mind*, Windhorse Publications, Birmingham 2001, pp.16–18.

31 See, for example, Harari, *Sapiens*, ch.5.

32 See Stuart Whatley, 'The myth of busyness', *Huffington Post* (25 September 2015), available at https://www.huffingtonpost.co.uk/entry/myth-of-busyness_us_55ffffc9e4b08820d91939cf, accessed on 1 October 2018.

33 Elizabeth Shove, *Comfort, Cleanliness, and Convenience: The Social Organisation of Normality*, Berg, Oxford 2003, pp.173ff.

34 Alvin Toffler, *Future Shock*, Pan Books, London 1971.

35 Toffler, *Future Shock*, p.20.

36 Toffler, *Future Shock*, p.45.

37 Toffler, *Future Shock*, p.30.

38 See https://en.wikipedia.org/wiki/Megacity, accessed on 1 October 2018.

39 See https://en.wikipedia.org/wiki/Megacity, accessed on 1 October 2018.

40 See https://ourfiniteworld.com/2012/03/12/world-energy-consumption-since-1820-in-charts, accessed on 1 October 2018.

41 Toffler, *Future Shock*, p.31.

42 For more on the problem of household waste, see www.worldwatch.org/global-municipal-solid-waste-continues-grow, accessed on 1 October 2018.

43 See https://www.theguardian.com/environment/2017/jun/28/a-million-a-minute-worlds-plastic-bottle-binge-as-dangerous-as-climate-change, accessed on 1 October 2018.

44 Tim Kreider, 'The "busy" trap', *New York Times* (30 June 2012). See also Elizabeth Kolbert, 'No time: how did we get so busy?', *The New Yorker* (26 May 2014).

45 David Loy and Linda Goodhew, 'Consuming time', in *Hooked*, ed. Stephanie Kaza, Shambhala Publications, Boston 2005, p.177.

46 How can I know the past and future don't exist?! Maybe I am claiming more than is reasonable or knowable here. There are philosophers and philosophical schools, both Buddhist and Western, that argue that all times exist. This is also the view of the 'block universe' theory in modern physics. So, strictly speaking, perhaps I should say that *right now* I can only experience the present. The past and future I cannot experience directly in the present; all I know of them is just memory or anticipation in the mind. Thanks to Ratnaguna for taking issue with me here!

47 I came across another fascinating example of this recently. Imagine you are sitting on an aisle seat in an aeroplane, looking down the aisle at the door to the pilots' cabin. As the

plane taxies towards, and then accelerates down, the runway, the aisle appears to be level, and the door directly ahead of you. A minute later, once the plane has taken off, the aisle now seems to be uphill and the door higher up than you are. That is what you see. But how has the visual information that your eyes are receiving changed? Relative to your seat, the aisle and the door are still in the same position, and there will be no difference in the way light will be reflected off them and into your retina. So why does it appear so different? (If you are on a plane and watch what happens, you will see the aisle is 'uphill' and you may also notice, simultaneously, a feeling of 'strangeness' about that perception.) The reason the aisle appears to be going uphill is not primarily to do with your eyes. In our inner ear we have a sense of balance, and that sense is telling the mind that we are tipped up. The mind doesn't then present us with two, incompatible sensations – a visually level aisle, and an impression of being leant backwards. What the mind does is adjust the visual image to match what your sense of balance is telling you. Your eyes provide certain information, but the mind then produces a radically altered visual perception, based on other information. We don't see what our eyes see; we see what our mind sees.

48 Vessantara, *Tales of Freedom: Wisdom from the Buddhist Tradition*, Windhorse Publications, Birmingham 2000, p.154.

49 You can read an account of the Buddha making exactly this kind of argument with a man called Potthapada, quizzing him as to which is his real self – that of the past, present, or future. See *Poṭṭhapāda Sutta*, in *Dīgha Nikāya*, trans. Maurice Walsh, Wisdom Publications, Somerville, MA 1995, pp.168–9.

50 *Lakṣaṇa* translates as something like 'mark' or 'characteristic'. The Buddha taught that all worldly things are marked by the three *lakṣaṇa*s; they are all unsatisfactory, all impermanent, and

all empty of fixed self. Chapter 8, 'Reflection time', looks in more detail at Buddhist reflection practices on the *lakṣaṇa*s.

51 *Dhammapada*, ch.11, verse 10, trans. Sangharakshita, Windhorse Publications, Birmingham 2001, p.58.

52 *Kṣānti* is Sanskrit; the Pali is *khanti*.

53 For more on the practice of forgiveness, see Paramabandhu Groves and Jed Shamel, *Mindful Emotion: A Short Course in Kindness*, Windhorse Publications, Cambridge 2017, ch.8.

54 I have altered the wording slightly. The original saying, from the Austrian psychiatrist Thomas Stephen Szasz, was: 'The stupid neither forgive nor forget; the naïve forgive and forget; the wise forgive but do not forget.'

55 *Mettā bhāvanā* translates as something like 'cultivation of loving-kindness'. It is a meditation practice designed to help us develop more positive emotion, stronger responses of friendliness and kindness to anyone we meet.

56 Self-*mettā*, showing ourselves understanding and kindness, can be a difficult issue for some Westerners. The driven, clock-watched 'style' of time described in chapters 2 and 3 arises out of the particular quality of relationship many Westerners have with themselves – needing to prove themselves and their self-worth, because of an underlying self-doubt or even self-hatred. It may be that, if we want to slow down, we will first need more self-*mettā*. The *mettā bhāvanā* meditation practice does indeed start with loving-kindness towards oneself. Likewise, the work of forgiveness requires loving-kindness towards ourselves and what we feel, as well as loving-kindness for others.

57 This story, and many other extraordinary and moving stories, can be found on The Forgiveness Project website. I would particularly recommend the audio recording of Bud Welch's reflections on the aftermath of the loss of his daughter. See www.theforgivenessproject.com, accessed on 1 October 2018.

58 Jayarava, *Time for a Change*, available at http://jayarava. blogspot.com.ee, accessed on 1 October 2018.

59 'The wind does not blow', in Jaan Kaplinski, *Through the Forest*, Harvill Press, London 1996, p.12.

60 'Eternity', in William Blake, *Complete Writings*, ed. Geoffrey Keynes, Oxford University Press, Oxford 1972, p.179.

61 Of course this doesn't justify 'taking the not given'!

62 Maitreyabandhu, *Life with Full Attention: A Practical Course in Mindfulness*, Windhorse Publications, Cambridge 2009.

63 See http://www.lwdwtraining.uk/uncatagorized/the-top-five-regrets-of-the-dying, accessed on 1 October 2018.

64 J.A. Baker, *The Peregrine*, HarperCollins, London 2010, p.36.

65 This is one of the 'Proverbs of hell' in 'The marriage of heaven and hell', in Blake, *Complete Writings*, p.151.

66 From 'The marriage of heaven and hell', in Blake, *Complete Writings*, p.154.

67 For more on such a mode of awareness, see Sangharakshita, *Living with Awareness: A Guide to the Satipaṭṭhāna Sutta*, Windhorse Publications, Cambridge 2003, p.129.

68 For a much more full and detailed approach to this way of practising, I would recommend Rob Burbea, *Seeing That Frees: Meditations on Emptiness and Dependent Arising*, Hermes Amara Publications, West Ogwell 2014.

69 The verses are adapted from my book *Buddhism: Tools for Living Your Life*, Windhorse Publications, Birmingham 2007, ch.1. I was originally inspired to write my version of the verses by a longer and more detailed version written by Vishvapani, and found at http://madhyamavani.fwbo.org/8/reminders. html, accessed on 1 October 2018. You will find other versions, including more 'traditional' ones, in many books that draw on Tibetan Buddhism.

70 *Dhammapada*, ch.9, verses 6 and 7, pp.48–9.

71 *Dhammapada*, ch.1, verse 6, p.14.

72 The Buddha often emphasized applying a reflection to both self and other when he taught. See, for example, the *Satipaṭṭhāna Sutta* (*Majjhima Nikāya* 10) or the *Upajjhathana Sutta* (*Aṅguttara Nikāya* 5.57), also known as 'The five things everyone should contemplate'. (The four reminders could also be seen as a later elaboration of these five contemplations of the Buddha.)

73 For more on 'wise attention', see Anālayo, *Excursions into the Thought-World of the Pali Discourses*, Pariyatti Press, Onalaska 2012, pp.193–202.

74 Saint Augustine, *Confessions*, trans. R.S. Pine-Coffin, Penguin, Baltimore, MD 1961, p.294.

75 Apparently, for speakers of Aymara (spoken in Peru), the past is spoken of as being *ahead* of us, whereas it is the future that lies *behind*. When you think about it, this makes just as much sense as our metaphorical ways of conceiving of past and future. In a very real sense, the future is creeping up on us from behind; we don't yet know what it looks like. Whereas, with the past, we can recall it and know it; it is, in that sense, spread out before us. For more on this, and the language of time in different cultures, see Panos Athanasopoulos, 'Language alters our experience of time', https://theconversation.com/language-alters-our-experience-of-time-76761?utm_source=New+Daily+Newsletter+Subscribers&utm_campaign=2745ab0364-EMAIL_CAMPAIGN_2017_06_13&utm_medium=email&utm_term=0_4675a5c15f-2745ab0364-81751533, accessed on 1 October 2018.

76 Daniel Rosenberg and Anthony Grafton, *Cartographies of Time*, Princetown Architectural Press, New York 2003.

77 The argument here is not exactly analogous to the preceding argument about colours, sounds, smells, etc. It is a similar line of argument in that both the sensory qualities and the sense

of past/future are subject-dependent. But, as we will see as
the argument progresses, time is even more fundamentally
subject-dependent in that it is one of the 'forms' by which we
have experience.

78 At this point someone might want to interject: you are
saying that 'now' is subject-dependent, that it depends on *my*
perspective. What about when I am with someone else, or a
whole group of people? We *all* experience things happening at
the same time; we all agree on what is past, present, or future.
Surely this demonstrates that the flow of time is real, not
merely subject-dependent? Those people gathered together,
however, all have similar kinds of minds, and therefore a
similar perceptual (and conceptual) apparatus of time. There
seems to be a 'now' that everyone experiences and shares.
And, yes, there *is* a shared experience, but it is still subject-
dependent. It still depends on a particular, shared, perceptual
apparatus; perhaps we could say that it is 'inter-subject-
dependent'. This can make it appear more objectively real than
it really is, and more separate from that group of perceiving
subjects. We will look at this more closely later in the chapter,
but, if you were with a group of animals, rather than humans,
they would have a different experience of time, more located
in a present, with less tendency to think backwards or
forwards into past or future. So whose time is more real: theirs
or yours? See also note 81.

79 Bryan Magee, *Confessions of a Philosopher: A Journey Through
Western Philosophy*, Phoenix, London 1998, p.154.

80 Adrian Barton, *A Brief History of the Philosophy of Time*, Oxford
University Press, New York 2013, pp.105–7.

81 In comparing an animal's sense of time with the 'tensed
time' that self-aware human beings have evolved, we might
want to argue along the following lines: given that humans
are so successful at explaining and predicting events and

processes in the world, doesn't this show that human time must correspond to reality, to how things actually are in themselves? In other words, doesn't it show that time as experienced by humans is objectively true and real, not just a human construct? Or doesn't it at least show that our sophisticated human understanding of tensed time is *more* true and real than the time of animals without self-consciousness? Well, yes and no. Perhaps our human idea of time does correspond more closely to how things are in themselves; it does enable us to understand life as a process of change, of growth and decay. Yet with this comes a distinctively human and abstract idea of 'me' in something we call 'time'. Time is still an idea, a mind-made construct by which we are able to conceive of change. But there isn't, actually, any *thing* called time. The idea, the conceptual apparatus, of time allows us to get closer to understanding the conditioned, contingent nature of the universe, and yet that conceptual apparatus, too, is conditioned and contingent.

82 You can read an instance of the Buddha pursuing this line of argument in the *Poṭṭhapāda Sutta*, p.167. In this sutta the Buddha speaks of three types of 'acquired self'. (This is the translator's rendering of the term *atta-paṭilābha*.) The first type of acquired self is that experienced in the *kāma-loka* (the realm of sense desire), the second is that experienced in the *rūpa-loka* (a realm of more refined and meditative consciousness in which craving and aversion are temporarily inoperative), and the third is that experienced in the *arūpa-loka* (a realm of even more refined and subtle consciousness).

83 Andrew Olendzki, *Untangling Self: A Buddhist Investigation of Who We Really Are*, Wisdom Publications, Somerville, MA 2016, p.120.

84 *Soṇadaṇḍa Sutta*, in *Dīgha Nikāya*, trans. Maurice Walsh, p.131.

85 Those familiar with the twelve *nidāna*s (or links) of dependent

origination (as illustrated on the outer rim of the wheel of life) will see that the process I have described in the text corresponds to links 7 to 10 of the *nidāna* sequence as follows: *nidāna 7 – feeling*: pleasure or pain, *nidāna 8 – craving (or aversion)*: pulling towards (or pushing away) the object identified with those feelings of pleasure or pain, *nidāna 9 – grasping*: how the mind then gets more intensely involved in the object, *nidāna 10 – becoming*: the resultant experience of self and time as being more or less tight and urgent.

86 We can pursue further this analogy of the two trains moving along parallel rails, taking it in the direction of Einstein's ideas about relativity. We only know the speed of the other train relative to ours. It *appears* to go faster or slower, according to the speed of our train. Someone might say: yes, but if our train stops, then we can see how fast the other train is *really* moving. We can see, for example, that it is moving eastwards at 50 miles per hour. This, however, is still only relatively true; the apparent speed and motion of that train is relative to us watching, to our 'frame of reference'. From another frame of reference, things will appear totally differently. For instance, from a point in space above the earth, we could see that the train is moving over the surface of the earth, whilst the whole planet rotates on its axis in the opposite direction. Relative to where we are watching from now, the train appears to be moving backwards, very fast, in a huge arc. Which of these two views is the correct one? Neither; or, put another way, both are true, but only within their given frame of reference. We could step back further into space and, from here, we see that, as well as spinning on its axis, the earth (with the train moving on its surface) is also hurtling in a great orbit round the sun. Step back again, and the earth, sun, and whole solar system are part of a spiralling galaxy, which is itself moving through vast space, part of a universe that is still expanding.

From each of these perspectives, the speed and motion of that train are completely different. The point here is that there is no absolute speed or motion; they can only ever be measured relative to an observer and their speed and motion – in other words, measured within a given frame of reference. And, crucially, if there is no absolute speed, then there can be no absolute time either. Things may change, but the rate they change at is *always* only relative to other things that are themselves changing. How fast or slowly things seem to change can only ever be measured relatively, within a given frame of reference. How fast or slowly time seems to go will be relative to how fast or slowly you are going. The idea of a real, objective time proceeding at a fixed, uniform rate is an illusion.

87 One translation of the *Araañña Sutta* has the Buddha encouraging his followers not to 'grieve over the past' or 'yearn for the future', but instead to 'live only in the present'. However, in two alternative translations this last phrase is translated as 'they survive on the present' or 'the present is sufficient for them'. I don't know Pali, but I suspect these are the more literal translations, whilst the first translator has gone further in putting the Buddha's words into modern idiom. However, either way, it is clear that the emphasis is on avoiding grasping or repelling, and practising mindfulness and contentment. The three translations consulted (all accessed on 1 October 2018) are: *Araañña Sutta, Saṃyutta Nikāya* 1.10, trans. Andrew Olendzki (available at www.accesstoinsight. org/tipitaka/sn/sn01/sn01.010.olen.html); trans. Thanissaro Bhikkhu (available at www.accesstoinsight.org/tipitaka/sn/ sn01/sn01.010.than.html); and trans. John D. Ireland (available at www.accesstoinsight.org/tipitaka/sn/sn01/sn01.010.irel. html).

88 *The Honeyball Sutta*, in *Majjhima Nikāya*, pp.201–6. The

Buddha named the teaching 'The honeyball' after his cousin Ananda likened hearing it to a man exhausted by hunger and weakness eating a sweet made of a ball of honey and finding it delectable.

89 One particular translation of Nagarjuna's *Mūlamadhyamakakārikā* can be found in Stephen Batchelor, *Verses from the Centre: A Buddhist Vision of the Sublime*, Riverhead Books, New York 2000; see especially pp.100 and 117.

90 For more meditations on time, and more discussion of the reality of the moment, see Burbea, *Seeing That Frees*, pp.346–9.

91 See Burbea, *Seeing That Frees*, and also Rob Burbea, 'Dependent origination, awareness, and time', a talk available at www.dharmaseed.org/teacher/210/talk/11120/, accessed on 1 October 2018.

92 *Attadanda Sutta* ('Arming oneself'), *Sutta Nipata* 4.15, trans. Andrew Olendzki, available at www.accesstoinsight.org/tipitaka/kn/snp/snp.4.15.olen.html, accessed on 1 October 2018.

93 Subhuti, 'The three myths of the spiritual life', available at http://madhyamavani.fwbo.org/10/threemyths.html, accessed on 1 October 2018. I have used slightly different terminology from Subhuti. His three myths are 'self-development' (which I refer to as 'development'), 'self-surrender' (which I have rendered as 'surrender'), and 'self-discovery' (which I have called 'emergence').

94 The stories of Asangha, Hakuin, Marpa, and Shinran are just four examples, taken from different Buddhist schools and traditions, that could, despite their differences in many details, be argued to fit the basic pattern of 'development' and then 'surrender', closely followed by 'emergence'.

95 Viktor E. Frankl, *Man's Search for Meaning*, Rider, London 2008.

96 Frankl, *Man's Search for Meaning*, p.82.

97 Frankl, *Man's Search for Meaning*, p.81.

98 For example, see the *Bhayabhevera Sutta*, in *Majjhima Nikāya*, trans. Bhikkhu Ñāṇamoli and Bhikkhu Bodhi, Wisdom Publications, Somerville, MA 2005, pp.105–7. The third knowledge attained by the Buddha was that he was now liberated from the taints of sense desire, desire for being, and ignorance.

99 Being able to see one's past lives and being able to observe the karmic destiny of other beings were considered in the Indian Buddhist tradition as mundane abilities; they didn't, in themselves, constitute an attainment of Enlightenment. However, as described in this sutta, the Buddha didn't just have some amazing psychic experiences; crucially he *understood* their significance and what such visions revealed about the nature of mind, and just how deeply and fundamentally our 'world' of experience is conditioned by greed, hatred, and delusion.

100 Vishvapani Blomfield, *Gautama Buddha: The Life and Teachings of the Awakened One*, Quercus, London 2012.

101 From 'Auguries of innocence', in Blake, *Complete Writings*, p.431.

102 The Buddha never claimed to be omniscient, or able to tell the future. In fact, he was often dismissive of those who did make such claims, or claims of similar psychic abilities. It was not that the Buddha thought such psychic feats weren't possible. It was more that, for him, they weren't the real point: they weren't essential to the attainment of Enlightenment. However, there are numerous occasions in the Pali canon where the Buddha did make predictions about someone's future destiny after they had died. He would be asked whether the deceased would find a good rebirth or a bad one, or whether the person was irreversibly on the path to Enlightenment and would not be reborn in this human realm at all. Perhaps these stories illustrate the power of the

Buddha's understanding of the workings of karma. But this ability wasn't *in itself* a necessary spiritual attainment.

103 The original incident that the story of the Buddha and the king is based upon is found in the *Cūḷadukkhakkhandha Sutta*, in *Majjhima Nikaya*, trans. Bhikkhu Ñāṇamoli and Bhikkhu Bodhi, pp.186–9. In the original incident, the Buddha is debating with some followers of an ascetic teacher, and they compare the happiness of the Buddha to that of King Bimbisara of Magadha. In other words, it is an imaginary scenario, made up for the purposes of the debate. Elsewhere I have heard this incident turned into a story about an actual meeting of the Buddha and a king, and I have used that story here, just because it is a good story! It isn't, however, canonical or an actual historical happening.

104 *Mahāparinibbāna Sutta*, in *Dīgha Nikāya*, trans. Maurice Walsh, pp.267–9.

105 Simone Weil, quoted in *The Plough Quarterly* 13 (summer 2017), p.30.

106 The original study was by J.M. Darley and C.D. Batson, '"From Jerusalem to Jericho": a study of situational and dispositional variables in helping behavior', *Journal of Personality and Social Psychology* 27:1 (1973), pp.100–8. A short summary can be found at http://www.spring.org.uk/2009/12/when-situations-not-personality-dictate-our-behaviour.php, accessed on 1 October 2018.

107 See Sangharakshita, *The Bodhisattva Ideal: Wisdom and Compassion in Buddhism*, Windhorse Publications, Birmingham 1999, p.202ff., for more on the discontinuity of path and goal, time, and timelessness.

108 Haiku by Basho, in *The Essential Haiku: Versions of Basho, Buson, and Issa*, trans. Robert Hass, Bloodaxe Books, Tarset 2013, p.29.

109 Friedrich Nietzsche, *A Nietzsche Reader*, ed. R.H. Hollingdale, Penguin, London 1977, p.278.

110 Fyodor Dostoevsky, *The Gambler*, trans. Hugh Alpin, Hesperus Classics, London 2006.

111 Ratnaguna, *The Art of Reflection*, Windhorse Publications, Cambridge 2010, p.36.

112 'Aubade', in Philip Larkin, *Collected Poems*, Faber and Faber, London 1998, pp.208–9.

113 We could even draw out a correspondence between this material and that of the last chapter. The mode of 'development' corresponds with having definite aims and aspirations, and also with living from the perspective of 'one day' – living with a sense of urgency and priority. The mode of 'emergence' corresponds with shunning goals and targets, and also with living from the perspective of '1,000 years' – living free of hopes and expectations. Again, a blending of both of these dimensions is what is needed.

114 See Dainin Katagiri, *Each Moment Is the Universe: Zen and the Way of Being Time*, ed. Andrea Martin, Shambhala Publications, Boston 2011, ch.15.

115 See, for example, Alan Burdick, 'Time is contagious: how to control the subjective experience of time', available at http://nautil.us/issue/45/powr/time-is-contagious, accessed on 1 October 2018, or David M. Eagleman, 'Brain time', available at https://www.edge.org/conversation/brain-time, accessed on 1 October 2018.

116 See, for example, Stephan Rechtschaffen, *Time Shifting: A Revolutionary New Approach to Creating More Time for Your Life*, Rider, London 1996.

117 Stephen R. Covey, *The Seven Habits of Highly Effective People*, Simon & Schuster, London 2004, p.145ff.

118 Jon Kabat-Zinn, *Full Catastrophe Living*, Dell Publishing, New York 1990, p.467.

119 *A Nietzsche Reader*, pp.273–4.

120 There is an interesting review of *Into Great Silence* at http://

www.decentfilms.com/articles/groning, accessed on 1 October 2018.

121 Mark C. Taylor, *Time Limits: Where Time Went and Why We Have So Little Left*, Yale University Press, New Haven, CT 2014, p.345.

Index

Introductory Note

References such as '178–9' indicate (not necessarily continuous) discussion of a topic across a range of pages. Wherever possible in the case of topics with many references, these have either been divided into sub-topics or only the most significant discussions of the topic are listed. Because the entire work is about 'free time', the use of this term (and certain others which occur constantly throughout the book) as an entry point has been minimized. Information will be found under the corresponding detailed topics.

Index

Index

Index

jobs 25–6, 34, 52–3, 136
journals 183, 187, 223
journeys 17, 20, 49, 69–70, 86–8, 146, 217
joy 16, 96, 108, 160, 162
  binding to ourselves 97–100

Kaplinski, Jaan 25, 90
karma 104, 210, 223
Karuna Trust 152
kindness 74, 83, 104, 114–15, 124, 127–8, 199, 214
kings 164–5, 223
kisses 96, 100
knots 20–1, 81, 84, 129, 182, 184

lakṣaṇas 79, 213–14
language 89, 91, 127–8, 135, 138, 141–3, 148, 216
leisure time 27, 35, 41, 44, 47, 52–3, 177
lens of impermanence 108–9, 113, 201, 203
life 17, 25–6, 83–7, 94–5, 97–107, 113–15, 160–3, 197–200
  Buddhist 135, 148
  human 41, 51, 55, 72, 87, 169–70, 179
  as precious opportunity 198
  spiritual 143–4, 146, 221
  winged 96–8
light 84, 102, 107–8, 112, 114, 119, 126, 213
  of awareness 74, 139, 178
lightness 108, 110, 114, 203
lightning conductor analogy 144, 148
longing 21, 93, 130–2, 136, 178
loving-kindness 78, 82, 101, 106, 108, 110, 174, 214

Man's Search for Meaning 150
maps 62, 121
meals 11, 24, 31–4
measurement, time 29, 87
mechanical timekeeping devices 28–9, 55, 87
meditation 20–1, 27, 78, 142–3, 146–7, 160, 189, 207
  on time 189–90
memories 62–4, 71, 74, 80, 117, 123, 193, 201
metaphors 40, 89–90, 144–9
  spatial 89, 118
middle 7, 86, 141, 171, 206
mind 37–9, 62–8, 104–7, 109, 112–13, 122–33, 200–205, 212–13
  state of 3, 11, 24, 121, 178
  time in the mind 119–24
mindfulness 15, 18, 135–6, 138, 152–3, 193, 202, 215
mindset 30, 182
mobile phones 27, 45–6, 70, 185
modern time 33, 54–5
modern world 43, 54
moments
  change at every moment 202–3
  of experience 112, 139, 206
  finding 139–42, 205–6
money 34–5, 52, 54, 152, 198
monks 147, 163, 189–90
mothers 77, 80
motion 13, 37–8, 86, 88, 219–20
motivation 79, 82, 102, 105
movements 90, 116, 137
musicians 111, 132, 165
mutability 99
mystery 115, 154, 161
myths 73, 95, 144–5, 192, 221

Index

Ñāṇamoli, Bhikkhu 222–3
natural cycles 29, 87–8
natural history 192
negative emotions 67, 71, 80, 83, 109, 151
Newton, Isaac 37
Newtonian view 37, 55
nidāna 218–19
nirvana 145
no self 75, 79, 124, 127–8
now time 135–57

objective time 87–8, 93–4, 121, 160, 179, 220
objects 61, 67, 91, 96–7, 112, 129–30, 142, 219
observers 2, 119–21, 179, 220
one day 169, 173–5, 186, 224
opportunity 66, 68, 102–3, 106, 171, 183, 198
oppression 3, 194
organic cycles 36
out there 26, 125, 128

pain 18–19, 21, 68–70, 73, 79, 81–4, 209–10, 219
Pali canon 163–4, 222
papañca 138
parents 77–80, 97, 103, 113, 200
passengers 31–2, 131–2
passing of time 33, 73, 88–91, 140, 179–80
past
  and different time-worlds 30–4
  and future 62, 138–9, 178–9, 190, 212, 216
  letting go of 142
path 103, 139, 143, 145–6, 148, 168, 222–3
patience 81, 157, 169

pausing 97, 103, 182, 208
pendulums 29, 87–8
perceptions 13, 44, 62–5, 71, 99, 122, 127, 162
  of time 15–17
  visual 63, 213
personality 104, 191, 210, 223
perspectives 102, 105, 168–9, 171, 173–5, 178, 217, 224
  evolutionary 66, 123
  temporal 75, 130
photograph 59
planes 20–1, 30–2, 133, 213
planet earth 85–6, 94
plants 42, 95, 149, 154
play time 174–94
plenitude 164–5, 168–9, 173, 175, 207
poems 25, 90, 96, 169, 196
polarization 129, 131, 175
population 35–6, 42–3, 49–50
possessions 24, 30, 97, 143, 147
possibility, dwelling in 153–4
power 36, 46, 105, 165, 222
preliminaries, four 102, 105, 107
present moment 19, 21, 135–6, 138–40, 142, 153, 205–7
  being in the 136, 138
  value 137–9
pressure 43–4, 143, 169
  time 14, 171, 184
proliferating thoughts 137–9
Protestant work ethic 35–6, 54
psychologists 12, 16, 62, 73
  social 166

quality
  of our attention 11, 23, 109, 178
  of our time 15, 23, 45, 53–4, 191
queues 1–2, 7, 31, 166

Index

WINDHORSE PUBLICATIONS

Windhorse Publications is a Buddhist charitable company based in the UK. We place great emphasis on producing books of high quality that are accessible and relevant to those interested in Buddhism at whatever level. We are the main publisher of the works of Sangharakshita, the founder of the Triratna Buddhist Order and Community. Our books draw on the whole range of the Buddhist tradition, including translations of traditional texts, commentaries, books that make links with contemporary culture and ways of life, biographies of Buddhists, and works on meditation.

As a not-for-profit enterprise, we ensure that all surplus income is invested in new books and improved production methods, to better communicate Buddhism in the 21st century. We welcome donations to help us continue our work – to find out more, go to windhorsepublications.com.

The Windhorse is a mythical animal that flies over the earth carrying on its back three precious jewels, bringing these invaluable gifts to all humanity: the Buddha (the 'awakened one'), his teaching, and the community of all his followers.

Windhorse Publications
17e Sturton Street
Cambridge CB1 2SN
UK
info@windhorsepublications.com

Perseus Distribution
210 American Drive
Jackson TN 38301
USA

Windhorse Books
PO Box 574
Newtown NSW 2042
Australia

THE TRIRATNA BUDDHIST COMMUNITY

Windhorse Publications is a part of the Triratna Buddhist Community, an international movement with centres in Europe, India, North and South America and Australasia. At these centres, members of the Triratna Buddhist Order offer classes in meditation and Buddhism. Activities of the Triratna Community also include retreat centres, residential spiritual communities, ethical Right Livelihood businesses, and the Karuna Trust, a UK fundraising charity that supports social welfare projects in the slums and villages of India.

Through these and other activities, Triratna is developing a unique approach to Buddhism, not simply as a philosophy and a set of techniques, but as a creatively directed way of life for all people living in the conditions of the modern world.

If you would like more information about Triratna please visit thebuddhistcentre.com or write to:

London Buddhist Centre
51 Roman Road
London E2 0HU
UK

Aryaloka
14 Heartwood Circle
Newmarket NH 03857
USA

Sydney Buddhist Centre
24 Enmore Road
Sydney NSW 2042
Australia